West of the Thirties

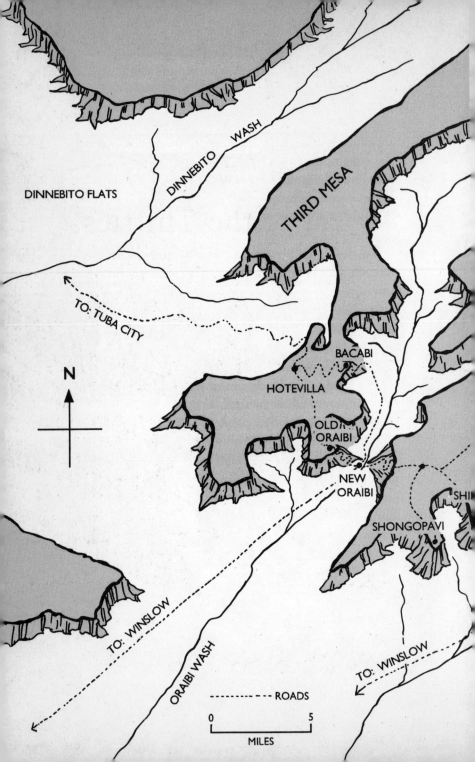

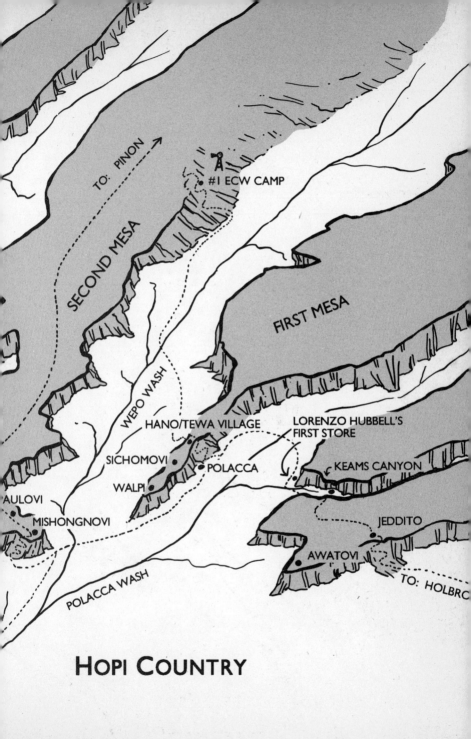

TO: PINON

#1 ECW CAMP

SECOND MESA

FIRST MESA

WEPO WASH

HANO/TEWA VILLAGE

LORENZO HUBBELL'S
FIRST STORE

SICHOMOVI

POLACCA

KEAMS CANYON

WALPI

AULOVI

MISHONGNOVI

JEDDITO

AWATOVI

POLACCA WASH

TO: HOLBRO

HOPI COUNTRY

Janice H. Marie 92

BOOKS BY EDWARD T. HALL

An Anthropology of Everyday Life: An Autobiography
1992

Understanding Cultural Differences
(with Mildred Reed Hall)
1990

Hidden Differences: Doing Business with the Japanese
(with Mildred Reed Hall)
1987

The Dance of Life: The Other Dimension of Time
1983

Beyond Culture
1976

The Fourth Dimension in Architecture:
The Impact of Building on Man's Behavior
(with Mildred Reed Hall)
1975

Handbook for Proxemic Research
1974

The Hidden Dimension
1966

The Silent Language
1959

West
of the
Thirties

DISCOVERIES
AMONG THE NAVAJO
AND HOPI

Edward T. Hall

ANCHOR BOOKS
DOUBLEDAY
New York London Toronto Sydney Auckland

An Anchor Book

PUBLISHED BY DOUBLEDAY

a division of Bantam Doubleday Dell Publishing Group, Inc.
1540 Broadway, New York, New York 10036

ANCHOR BOOKS, DOUBLEDAY, and the portrayal of an anchor are
trademarks of Doubleday, a division of Bantam Doubleday Dell
Publishing Group, Inc.

West of the Thirties was originally published in
hardcover by Doubleday in 1994.

Library of Congress Cataloging-in-Publication Data

Hall, Edward Twitchell, 1914–
West of the thirties : discoveries among the Navajo and Hopi
Edward T. Hall.—1st Anchor Books ed.
        p.   cm.
Originally published: New York: Doubleday, 1994.
Includes bibliographical references and index.
1. Navajo Indians.   2. Hopi Indians.   3. Hall, Edward Twitchell, 1914–
4. Anthropologists—Arizona—Biography.   5. Arizona—
Description and travel.   I. Title.
[E99.N3H273   1995]
973′.04972—dc20   94-36043
        CIP

ISBN 0-385-42422-1
Copyright © 1994 by Edward T. Hall
All Rights Reserved
Printed in the United States of America
First Anchor Books Edition: February 1995

1   3   5   7   9   10   8   6   4   2

This book is dedicated to Lorenzo Hubbell, second-generation Indian trader, friend and mentor, who grew up as Spanish, Navajo, Hopi, and Anglo-American. Sharing the real-life experience of four cultures, he set me straight as to the true meaning of accommodation and understanding.

Contents

Maps and Illustrations

Opening map: Hopi country.

INTRODUCTION
OPENING PHOTO: Navajo camp. Parkhurst, ca. 1935, neg. #3103. *(Courtesy of Museum of New Mexico)*

HALF TITLE: Model-A Ford in Steamboat Wash. *(Hall)*

CHAPTER 1: **Keams**
OPENING PHOTO: Keams Canyon trading post. Wittick, ca. 1885–95, neg. #16473. *(Courtesy of School of American Research, Collections in the Museum of New Mexico)*
CLOSING PHOTO: Navajos in wagon. Parkhurst, ca. 1935, neg. #43140. *(Courtesy of Museum of New Mexico)*

CHAPTER 2: **My Navajo Name**
OPENING PHOTO: Author's Jeddito cabin (no space for washbasin inside). *(Hall)*
CLOSING PHOTO: Author with his Model-A Ford. *(Minton)*

CHAPTER 3: **Lorenzo**
OPENING PHOTO: Lorenzo's Oraibi trading post. *(Hall)*
CLOSING PHOTO: Lorenzo Hubbell. *(Hall)*

CHAPTER 4: **The Experience of Place**
OPENING PHOTO: Hopi village of Walpi. Vroman, 1895, neg. #V-512(622). *(Courtesy of Seaver Center for Western History Research, Natural History Museum of Los Angeles County)*
CLOSING PHOTO: Monument Valley. *(Hall)*

CHAPTER 5: **The Hopis**
OPENING PHOTO: Supela, Walpi Snake Priest. Vroman, 1900, neg. #V-2376(C26). *(Courtesy of Seaver Center for Western History Research, Natural History Museum of Los Angeles County)*

CHAPTER 6: **The Fragility of Understanding**
OPENING PHOTO: Two Navajos on horseback. *(Hall)*
CLOSING PHOTO: Navajo man with jug. *(Hall)*

CHAPTER 7: **The Navajos**
OPENING PHOTO: Navajos and hogan at Bitahooche. Vroman, 1895, neg. #V-710. *(Courtesy of Seaver Center for Western History Research, Natural History Museum of Los Angeles County)*
CLOSING PHOTO: Hogan. *(Hall)*

CHAPTER 8: **The Government in Sheep's Clothing**
OPENING PHOTO: Navajo Country. *(Hall)*
CLOSING PHOTO: Navajo Service pickup with Navajos in the back. *(Unknown)*

CHAPTER 9: **The Trading Business**
OPENING PHOTO: Typical trading post. Snow, ca. 1949, neg. #46809. *(Courtesy of Museum of New Mexico)*

Acknowledgments

NO MATTER what people think, the writing and production of a book is inevitably the result of a team process. Because of the great time span—as well as the changes in the three cultures described in this book—it was rewritten several times. The problems to be solved in translating from the tacit dimensions of one or more cultures to another are enormous. They complicate everything: writing, editing, copy editing, as well as the micro details of style and the actual picture of language, which we carry in our heads. It is at this point that one begins to learn again and again all the little things that are taken for granted in our culture but which do not occur in another.

Writing a book is, among other things, a matter of relationships, one of the most important of which is the link between the author and his/her agent. In this regard I have been singularly blessed by the presence of a strong, supportive, and gifted friend Jill Kneerim, of the Palmer Dodge agency. Knowing she was in my corner has not only been reassuring but has given me the peace of mind so essential to creative work. I want to thank her for every-thing she has done to make this book happen.

Concerning the transformation of my manuscript into the book which you hold in your hands, my first acknowl-edgment is to my Doubleday editor, Martha Levin, pub-lisher of Anchor books, and her deputy Deborah Acker-man. I am particularly grateful to my friend, and former Doubleday editor, the author Jake Page for his contribu-tions to the final version of this book. I owe thanks to Sally Arteseros, who was my long-time Doubleday editor, and to Jana Oyler, friend, stylistic consultant, and editor, who worked on earlier versions of the manuscript. I don't think it would have been possible to produce this volume with-out the active participation and help of my assistant Karen Josey. Her talent, dedication, and sensitively applied intel-ligence in handling permissions, matters of format and style, and her skills in the process of transforming a typed manuscript into final form ready for publication made my job much easier than I had expected. I will be forever grateful.

I also wish to acknowledge and thank the following in-stitutions for their generosity in the use of photographs from their archives: the Seaver Center for Western History Research, the Natural History Museum of Los Angeles County, California, the School of American Research, and the Museum of New Mexico in Santa Fe.

I also wish to thank Mildred Reed Hall, my wife, life-long partner, and friend for her untiring support in this enterprise.

My last and most important acknowledgment is to the Hopi and the Navajo People, who have long endured the pain of not being understood. As always my hope is that in writing this book, my own people will comprehend a little of what it means to be Indian, and some of what is involved in appreciating their brothers and sisters who are different and in so doing accept them with love in their hearts. I say this as a reminder that the world's greatest—as yet to be tapped—resource is to be found in its ethnic diversity.

INTRODUCTION
The Country and Its People

A BOOK'S TITLE should indicate something about what the reader will find between its covers. *West of the Thirties* was a deliberate choice, conjuring up both space and time to suggest something mysterious. For Americans and many others "The West" has always evoked romantic images of vast, open spaces—a frontier. "The Thirties," on the other hand, represents a temporal watershed in which the shape of the world to come was far from clear. A time remembered by most through the herky-jerk of black-and-white movies, calling up images of the Great Depression, the Dust Bowl, shelterbelts, contour plowing, people selling apples on the streets, hoboes riding the rails, songs like "The Big Rock Candy Mountain," and lines of men seeking jobs. But by the thirties, the West was for the most part thoroughly settled. Roads, automobiles, telephones, radios —all had served to tame the Old West. In what had been frontier, everything was now, as the song put it, "up-to-date."

From 1933 to 1937, I lived in a country within a country, a place where the trappings of modernity were barely visible—the Navajo and Hopi reservations. It was a place where time had almost stood still, an enormous area— 280,000 square miles, 250 miles from east to west, 180 miles from north to south—located mostly in northeastern Arizona but spilling over into New Mexico and Utah. A land of red rock, mesas, buttes, spires, vast stretches of semiarid grasslands, and cut by dry arroyos transformed into torrents when it rained. This Indian country contained some of the most spectacular scenery in North America. And at the time it was the least known, least visited, and least understood part of the United States.

In its approximate middle were the remote village-dwelling Hopis—some five thousand persons living in a dozen villages mostly perched, like medieval towns, on three mesas high above the surrounding desert. The village of Oraibi (sometimes called old Oraibi) was thought to be the oldest continuously settled village or town in the United States. The trash mounds cut by the road at the edge of the village contained black-on-gray potsherds dating back more than a thousand years. The Hopis were sedentary people who tilled the soil, though *till* is not quite the correct word. Instead of plowing, they used digging sticks to make a hole some twelve inches deep, down to where there was moisture, and then dropped seeds into the hole. In this way they preserved the integrity of the soil and the moisture, along with the sparse surrounding ground cover.

The much more populous Navajos were semisedentary pastoralists who lived in small camps, far from one another. A typical camp consisted of one or more traditional forked poles (tepee-shaped) and the more recent octagonal dwellings called a *hogan*, a shade house made of branches, with a corral to the side. One of the most characteristic traits of the hogan was that the door always faced east. Most of this land was devoted to supporting Navajo stock; herds of horses and cattle and flocks of sheep and goats totaled between three hundred thousand and four hundred thousand head of grazing animals. Related to the Apaches, the Navajos are of Athapaskan stock. The Athapaskans, an important group, still live for the most part in Canada and Alaska. First entering the Southwest about one hundred years ahead of the Spanish, who came in 1540, the Navajos are the most recent Indian arrivals on the North American continent.

In the thirties there were few roads, only tracks left by the Indians' wagons, and no bridges to span the arroyos. Apart from a few anthropologists and early explorers, such as Adam Vroman, John Hillers, Edward S. Curtis, and a handful of Indian traders, no one really knew much of anything about the Indians or their country. In fact, one of my "discoveries" was how little most people—even the ones who lived there—knew about the first Americans. One of the chief characteristics of life on the reservation was that getting anywhere involved traveling endless miles either on marginal roads or simply following wagon tracks across the semidesert landscape. In winter the trip from

Oraibi to the railroad town of Winslow some ninety miles south might as well have been an expedition to the moon. One hundred fifty miles north of the Santa Fe Railroad connecting the towns of Gallup, Holbrook, Winslow, and Flagstaff was John Wetherill's Kayenta trading post, which housed the United States post office farthest from a railroad in the entire country. It was a five-hour drive from Kayenta to "Flag" in dry weather and a slippery, risky two-day trip in rain or snow. The memory of slipping and sliding over the top of the red-clay trail is still vividly etched in my mind. Every mile was an adventure.

It was still the *frontier*—of unimaginable scale, immense distances, expansive views, and incredible landscapes, ranging from an almost bare ground covering miles and miles of country to the spruce and aspen forest on Navajo Mountain in Utah. Most impressive, perhaps, was the freedom from all traces of "civilization." In certain places it was possible to look out over more than a hundred miles of empty, untouched landscape as God had made it. There were people out there, but somehow they didn't intrude on that magnificent scene. Because much of the country was still unexplored by whites, in \the Tsegi Marsh Pass area northwest of Kayenta, where I was doing an archaeological survey, there was no doubt in my mind that there had to be at least a few places where mine were the first footprints made by an American of European heritage.

From the moment I first set foot on the reservation, it was as though someone had turned on a switch in my head. I was transported out of myself through Lewis Carroll's looking glass to a distant, unfamiliar time and place —a world without boundaries, a world apart, cut off from the outside much as the surface of a habitable moon would be. Despite the strangeness, I felt safe, protected by an invisible shield from the outside world and the people in it. Deep inside I knew that my fate and this country were linked in some ineffable way.

I first visited Indian land in 1932. I was eighteen, it was summer, and I was earning money doing various odd jobs in Santa Fe, where I had lived since my parents' divorce in 1927. This particular summer, after my freshman year at Pomona College and a year abroad, a man I knew, Charley Minton, and I decided to drive across the reservation to the Grand Canyon in my 1929 Model-A Ford roadster. I loaded up with water, gas, oil, bedrolls and other supplies and set out for Gallup, New Mexico. Seven miles north of Gallup, at a place called Gamerco, a dirt road left the Gallup-Shiprock highway and entered the reservation, leading to Fort Defiance, which at the time was the primary Indian Service headquarters for the Navajo Reservation.

We drove through the rolling landscape of piñon, juniper, and sagebrush; after passing through Fort Defiance, we climbed Defiance Plateau through a beautiful forest of western yellow pine and ponderosa on a graded dirt road wide enough for two cars to pass. Beyond, down in piñon-juniper country again, lay J. L. Hubbell's trading post in Ganado and, beyond that, Keams Canyon, the Indian Service headquarters for the Hopi Reservation. Six miles west of Ganado, the road dwindled to a barely visible wagon track, turning the drive to Keams in the dark into a nerve-racking, uncertain ordeal. I found myself in a situation where there was no sure way of telling where I was going. Wagon tracks took off in all directions, making it difficult to determine which of them was the most traveled way to the west. Roads, as I understood the word, were nonexistent. I had depended on there being at least rudimentary signs tacked to a slender leaning post. But there were none.

Apparently the reservation dwellers, who knew their way around, didn't think it necessary to help the tenderfoot newcomer find his way. It was a little like being in the middle of the ocean in a small craft. From Ganado on, I navigated by dead reckoning and intuition. I can still remember sitting bolt upright, gripping the steering wheel, craning my neck, and squinting to be sure I didn't miss any significant clues. Charley, a St. Louis attorney, sat next to me like a bump on a log, totally oblivious to our situation and to the problems I was having to solve. In fact, I have seldom felt so alone and isolated as I did in a pitch-black surround with a tiny arc of light bouncing in front of me while I followed two winding ruts through an endless sea of sagebrush, piñon, and juniper trees. I could tell by the stars and my own sense of direction that we were heading west, but into what?

After a couple of hours, we were still headed west and I was beginning to feel more secure. At least we hadn't ended up at some hogan (Navajo dwelling). Then, without warning we were in the soup. Three hours out of Ganado, we were confronted with what looked like a few inches of water in the Steamboat Wash, a narrow arroyo with a steep clay bank facing us that must be climbed on the other side. I stopped, surveyed the situation, and decided to use a procedure that had always stood me in good stead when crossing streams in New Mexico. With seventy-five or so yards of straight approach to the arroyo, I knew I could get up enough momentum to carry me over the top of the precipitous bank on the other side. I disconnected the fan belt, so the fan wouldn't spray water on the ignition and kill the engine. I backed up, put the car in low gear, and floorboarded it, plunging into the wash with enough momentum to carry me up the opposite bank. When I hit the wash, a huge fan-shaped spray of muddy water was followed a split second later by a horrendous jolt. The front wheels hit and then bounced over an unexpected, invisible obstruction at the base of the far bank. An examination revealed that the car's front end was intact, which was a break. But we were still ignominiously stuck. The front wheels were halfway up the bank while the muddy water swirled around the rear wheels, mired above the hubcaps in gray clay. There was nothing to do except wait until morning. Out with the bedrolls and into the sack.

In the morning a Navajo in a wagon came along. He didn't speak English, so I gestured and he gestured and then he unhitched his team and pulled us out. The rescue cost us five 1930s dollars. Once free of the mud, we bounced across the country along wagon tracks we had been following the night before. This course would carry us past Jeddito, Keams Canyon, and the Hopi villages of Polacca and Mishongnovi.

In Oraibi we stopped to meet the famous Indian trader Lorenzo Hubbell. His store stood in the middle of a bare, shadeless space in the center of New Oraibi (now called Kyakotsmovi). Parking in the intense sunlight, we entered his office via a porch through a side door. It was like entering a movie theater. Once our eyes had adjusted to the low light level, we could see several people sitting around in chairs and a heavyset man behind a desk who greeted us in a gravelly voice with "I'm Lorenzo Hubbell. Please sit down. Which way did you come?" We sat there for thirty minutes while Lorenzo conducted business with a variety of people, orchestrating perhaps a dozen transactions from behind his desk. Even during that short visit, I sensed the power of this man's magnetic presence.

After getting Hubbell's directions to Tuba City, west of

New Oraibi, we drove to the Hopi town of Hotevilla and then on to the other side of the Dinnebito Wash, where we headed north and west toward Blue Canyon. We drove in a narrow, deep gorge barely wide enough for a small vehicle or wagon to the trading post at Red Lake. The walls of Blue Canyon were so steep that if I had been unlucky enough to get caught in the frequent floodwaters, they would have meant certain death. There was no way out. My heart was in my mouth for the entire duration of that fifty or so mile stretch. At Red Lake, an isolated trading post in the middle of a parched open space, we finally had the luxury of driving again on a graded gravel road with signs and other amenities of civilization. I had never thought of a road sign as an amenity, but having succeeded in getting around without them, I no longer take them for granted. At Cameron on the way to the Grand Canyon, we left the reservation. I calculated that with zigs and zags and a little wheel spinning in the mud, we had traveled over three hundred miles in two days in Indian territory. Those three hundred miles were like traveling on another planet.

It was a planet I would get to know much better.

What I would see was no Fred Harvey Indian Detour for rich tourists cradled in the luxury of a Cadillac limousine, insulated from reality as they imposed their fantasies on the passing scene from the other side of the car window. I came to know the reality of reservation life with all its various players. Droughts were so serious and long-lasting that the specter of starvation was a permanent feature in the makeup of every Hopi's psyche, a psychology of scarcity and caution that whites had trouble understanding. On issues regarding reservation life, the United States Government behaved like a mad, unpredictable stepmother from a Grimm folktale, and the Indian Service, the local representative of the government, was entrenched in bureaucratic detail and staffed by disaffected employees. The Indian traders were the information centers and the economic hub of what wealth there was, which formed the basis of a complex interplay of the reservation's four cultures—Navajo, Hopi, Hispanic, and Anglo.

For the next four years I lived in what would be the last gasp of the nineteenth century, and I would never be the same again. Thanks to Lorenzo Hubbell, the trader at New Oraibi who actually tutored me, as did the Indians, I was able to truly understand matters I would never have otherwise made sense of. Lorenzo's method was to tell me stories to illuminate as well as to instruct. The Navajos and the Hopis also had stories to tell, their own personal stories as well as stories passed down from their ancestors.

These stories did not start when I first set foot on Indian soil. In telling me their stories, people were explaining themselves as products of their past. Some of those stories have by now been recorded and appear in print. Others have not and will be lost forever. At that time, however, they were merely part of the oral history of the country.

I didn't actually witness the indignity forced on the Hotevilla Hopis as they were deloused by white government officials who ran them through a sheep-dip full of Black Leaf 40 (nicotine). And I only heard about the early-eighteenth-century destruction of the greatest of all Hopi villages, Awatovi, by their own people. Nor was I there at the time of Lorenzo's uncle's murder by Navajos, or when Kit Carson rounded up the Navajos at the end of the Civil War and marched them to Fort Sumner, New Mexico *(Bosque Redondo)*. Interning the Navajos at Bosque Redondo was a brutal and an inhuman incident in which Navajos died of starvation because they didn't know—and were not told—how to prepare the white man's food. But because there were Indians who had lived through these times or had been told about them as children, the stories and their associated indignities were kept alive and became a part of my reservation experience. One old Navajo man I knew was famous because he had "killed lots of white men." Almost without exception, the Indians were still full of these experiences, reacting to whites in response to the rich, violent, and mad reality of our shared past.

This, then, is a story of discovery in another age—an age long past.

The West of the thirties is gone now, vanished without a trace. Only vivid images of those extraordinary times are real in my mind's eye and the eyes of the few who are left. So, try to imagine a place with no roads, no radios (they were available but people didn't use them), no bridges, only the most primitive automobiles: Where the Indians got around on foot, on horseback, and in wagons. Where it was possible to drive for an entire day and not see another human being. When the attitudes toward Indians held by most whites were framed by convictions that the Indians were inferior and that the only solution was to make them over in the white man's image. Yet when one penetrated beneath the surface of that world, there was a truth, a veracity, which is difficult if not impossible to find today. The Indians, particularly the Navajos, were still themselves and relatively untouched by the white man's culture; only a handful of the fifty thousand spoke English.

So, this is a look at the life and the country that lay "west of the thirties"—the land and the peoples that once lived it as well as the indelible imprint it left on the life of a young anthropologist.

West of the Thirties

1

Keams

ONE DAY Lorenzo Hubbell, the trader at Oraibi, told me this story. At the time it took place, in 1906, Lorenzo was in his twenties and owned the store at Keams Canyon.

For some time, trouble had been brewing between two factions of the Hopis, the *Friendlies,* who wanted to cooperate with the white man—for example, by sending their children to white-run schools—and the *Hostiles,* who didn't want to have anything to do with the white world. There was bickering over ceremonies, government-sponsored disputes over land below the mesas, attempts to rid the villages of one another, and a few outright acts of internal violence. The center of the controversy was at Oraibi, but it had spread to the villages on other mesas. Yet another problem was with the Navajos, who would occasionally steal crops and stock and were encroaching on Hopi springs. As a result there were eruptions here and there on the mesas. The ancient troubles—severe raiding between the Hopis and the Navajos—had greatly abated since the 1880s, when the government's presence on the reservation was established. But only seven years earlier, in 1899, some Navajos had fallen upon a Hopi man near Oraibi and killed him. There now was a kind of truce between the two tribes (and considerable interaction), but it was an uneasy truce at best.

All this was known by Theodore G. Lemmon, the superintendent of the Indian Agency in Keams Canyon. A severe-looking man with close-cropped hair and an enormous spade-shaped beard, he had arrived in these precincts the year before at a time when relations between the hostiles and the government had reached a state of undeclared war.

In January 1906, in defiance of the superintendent's latest demands that their children go to the white-run schools, a number of Hopi men had gone into the underground chambers called *kivas,* where ceremonial activity and planning took place. They refused to come out. To show them who was boss, Lemmon tried unsuccessfully to force them out and then hit on what seemed to him to be a splendid idea. He would hire the Navajos to do it. The Navajos were only too happy to help, but then Lemmon vacillated, holding the Navajos in check down below the mesa as though they were on leashes. The superintendent could have done nothing worse than vacillate; uncertainty and indecision had always been an anathema to the Navajos. After days of inaction, Lemmon called them off altogether and paid them—but in script, notes that simply said the government owed them a certain amount of money.

Later, the Navajos went to Lorenzo's trading post to spend their script, and he had to tell them he couldn't accept it, that only real money was good at the store.

The Navajos went wild. One of the headmen, with his horse rearing, waved his piece of paper in the air and shouted, *"Sl'not-sos, Do ya shonda; sl'not-sos, Do ya shonda!"* ("The paper is no good, the paper is no good!") Once started on something, a Navajo is obliged to finish it; they had to act. In no time the Navajos decided that since they had been denied the satisfaction of engaging the Hopis and hadn't even been paid, there was no choice but to go to the agency, pull Lemmon out of his house, put him in a buckboard, take him to the top of the hill outside Keams Canyon, and send him on his way to Winslow.

But Lorenzo intervened. He ran out of the store and grabbed the reins of the rearing horse of the still-shouting Navajo headman. Speaking in their language, he calmed the Navajo leader and persuaded him to give up his plan. It was an act of considerable courage, requiring a great deal of resourcefulness and a deep understanding of the ways of the Navajos, something that was in severely short supply among the non-Indians on the reservation in those days. Superintendent Lemmon left a year later, never knowing that Hubbell had saved him this indignity—and perhaps his life.

Less than three decades later, I was thrust into this still-resonating force field.

In 1933, toward the end of my sophomore year at college (I had transferred to the University of Denver and discovered the field of anthropology), I received a telegram out of the blue from John Collier, the new commissioner of Indian Affairs in Washington, D.C., offering me a job "working on an Indian reservation as part of a new and innovative program." I leaped at the chance and accepted immediately. I didn't know the new commissioner personally, but I had been friends with his sons, whom I first met at Indian dances like the large Corn Dance at Santo Domingo. I assumed that consistent with the New Deal instituted by Franklin D. Roosevelt, Collier, who had been a leader in the Indian rights movement, wanted to inject new blood into the system. I was right. Later, waiting around in Santa Fe, I eventually learned that I was slated to be a "camp manager" for the Indian equivalent of the Civilian Conservation Corps (CCC).

Run by the Army, Roosevelt's CCC camps taught young men such skills as welding, carpentry, auto mechanics, and masonry—skills the CCC put to work building and maintaining trails, campgrounds, administrative buildings, and roads, mostly in the national forests. The work was practical, designed to improve the forests and their facilities as well as the individuals being trained. Many unemployed youths, young men, and heads of families from all parts of the country—including the cities—were literally dumped in the middle of the national forests and put to work. The program included instruction in reading and writing, a dose of discipline, and practical experience with the basic skills of outdoor maintenance, cement work, and general construction, and provided a small stipend. The Indian version of the CCC camps were designed to improve the country by building roads, dams, and so forth on the reservations. As a way of providing work for the Indians, it was to be run by civilians instead of by the Army.

In July word came that I was to report to Superintendent

Edgar Miller at Keams Canyon, Arizona. Since the Hopi Reservation had been my first choice from the beginning, I was delighted. Two days later I was sitting in my car on a narrow road, looking down into Keams Canyon at the agency buildings strung out between yellowish gray sandstone canyon walls. About eighty miles north of Holbrook, Keams Canyon was far from prepossessing; it still looked the way it had the year before: hot, dusty, and forbidding. The Indian Service had originally been established by the Army, and the agency at Keams had a somber, depressing aura, which reflected its military antecedents. The squat buildings were all made from the local Wingate sandstone, but unlike the flat-roofed trading posts, the agency buildings had peaked roofs covered with green tar paper, the stamp of an alien presence.

The agency proper, I soon learned, was made up of a headquarters, a school for Indian children, dormitories and dining halls for boys and girls, a hospital with a staff of three doctors and a half dozen nurses, and a dismal-looking jail with a steel door and iron bars, located on the ground floor of one of the main buildings. In addition, there were employee housing units, recreational facilities, and a garage for maintaining government vehicles. Nearby, to the west, was the United States Irrigation Service, responsible for drilling wells and developing springs on the reservation. And farther west, around a bend in the road, lay Slim Halderman's trading post, the same post where Lorenzo Hubbell had begun his trading career at age 19 at the beginning of the century.

In low gear, I half slid down the narrow road that hugged the precipitous side of the canyon, crossed Keams Wash, and found my way to the center of the compound and the squat stone structure that was the agency administration building. Waiting there to check in, I sat on a bench outside Miller's office for nearly an hour. A second office belonged to Keeley, the chief clerk, who was responsible for agency regulations and also for dispensing funds. I never did learn Keeley's first name, because no one ever used it. I didn't see Keeley that first day, but he turned out to be a large, unpleasant man with the pasty pallor of old biscuit dough. Whenever he would emerge like a badger from his hole, the clerks occupying ranks of desks outside his office door would bend their heads even lower. He had been the superintendent of a reservation in Oregon and had succumbed to his libidinal drives and the wiles of one of the local young Indian women. Discovered, he was demoted from superintendent to clerk and had now worked his way up to the number-two position, which, with its power of the purse, had considerable influence. Woe to anyone who crossed him. He didn't bother to conceal his hatred of Indians, intellectuals, outsiders, and anyone not under his thumb. Later he managed to do me out of 7 percent of a year's salary by failing to authorize payment for mileage on my car, which he had asked me to use as a convenience to the government. Keeley, being Keeley, had failed to put through the proper paperwork to Washington!

Having cooled my heels outside Miller's office, I was surprised when I finally met him. I had in my mind's eye someone like the clean-cut, well-turned-out park rangers at the Grand Canyon National Park I had met the previous summer. Instead here was a little gnome with a red face and beady eyes, a bulbous nose, ears that stuck out, and patches of gray hair on a balding scalp. He was hunched over, tense, with a hint of weasel in his demeanor. He was clearly suspicious of me—an outsider hired by Collier, no less—and far from friendly. He didn't get up when I entered nor did he shake my hand, which in the West was a clear rebuff. It was obvious early on that he didn't like the crew of the New Deal—a program to be run by strangers and over which he had little or no control.

I had expected to receive some description of my job, maybe even something about his relations with the Hopis, but here again I was surprised. He told me simply that I was new on the reservation and to *"stay away from the Indian traders."* He said that if I went outside and looked down toward the arroyo, I would see some tents where I would find the people I would be working with. That was all he said.

I went out wondering what the warning about the traders was all about. What did it mean? It made no sense to me; from my visit to Hubbell's the previous summer, it seemed that trading posts were where all the reservation action was. Fifty yards off, near Keams Wash, I came to some pitched tents and a small group of men standing around. A slick-looking character detached himself from the group, offered a limp hand, and told me he was Harry Masterson and that he was in charge. I later found out that he was an engineer who had been relieved of a cushy job in the Department of Commerce. He told another man, a young engineer, to brief me and show me to my tent.

Our tents were small, barely accommodating two army cots and a small table for a washbasin. The tents were under some cottonwood trees next to the wash and well out of sight of the administration building. Everything said we were not part of the regular scheme of things and we were to stay out of the agency's hair—except at mealtimes, when we ate at Keams Canyon headquarters in the community dining room. Meals were pretty awful. Breakfast consisted of canned fruit or juice, pancakes half an inch thick and covered in thick corn syrup, sausage, and boiled coffee left over from God knows what war. Fresh vegetables were a thing of the past; we had meat and potatoes with gray gravy.

Our little group came from all over and with the exception of myself, all were old government hands who had been "riffed"—reduced in force—from other government agencies in a move to cut expenses. None of the others seemed to know much about Indians. Since word had gotten around that there were other government jobs to be had, men sent in applications stating their qualifications. One applicant (fortunately he was not hired) wrote: "I know how to swing a baseball bat and can handle any Indian." Reading his letter, written in pencil with a childish scrawl, I was amazed. I thought such attitudes had gone with the passing of the nineteenth century.

Altogether there were only eight of us: a supervisor for the entire job, two engineers, a supervisor for all camps who would be my direct superior, a missionary to the Hopis who was a clerk-bookkeeper, a carpenter, a mechanic, and myself. It didn't take long to find out there were no camps for me to manage. In fact, no work of any kind was under way and no one seemed really interested in starting any. Not only that, there were no Hopis or Navajos on the payroll. So I set about getting acquainted and finding out what went on in the agency. I soon learned that I had been plunked down on the remote frontier of a bureaucracy and that the greater the distance from the centers of power, the more lax things became. Fortunately, there were a few people in our group with whom I could talk. One was a smooth, amiable man named MacCurtain, my direct boss.

Mac, it turned out, was heir to the hereditary chieftaincy of the Choctaws, one of the "five civilized tribes" that were relocated from the lower Mississippi states to reservations in Oklahoma, but he looked, dressed, talked, and acted like any other educated male from Oklahoma. As a boss, he didn't interfere but let people learn on their own, a trait I later recognized as characteristic of many Indians I have known. Mac, who arrived about a week after I did, earned the unheard-of salary of $2,880 a year. His wife, Eleanor, part Cherokee, was red-haired and curvaceous with freckled pale white skin. Both she and Mac drank a lot and liked a good time. It soon became apparent that their problem with alcohol was not unusual.

One afternoon I found the tent area in turmoil. Mac had gotten hold of his salary check before Eleanor could intercept it, and he had taken off for one of the railroad towns where he could buy liquor. Eleanor said that not only would he blow the entire check, but he was apt to do unpredictable things when drunk. She mobilized us males to go look for him; we decided to look in Winslow rather than Holbrook, since Winslow was larger. Today it is difficult to describe adequately what such a trip entailed. The automobiles then were at best fragile, cantankerous machines that could give up the ghost without pretext or notice. The main arteries to the railroad towns could hardly be called roads. There were ruts, mud holes, sand dunes, and rocks; the most rugged trucks could be shaken apart in a matter of weeks from driving over those roads. So the eighty- to ninety-mile trek—up to four hours long—was not to be taken lightly.

We found Mac's sedan about forty miles from Keams Canyon, not far from an isolated trading post due east of a basalt formation known as Giant's Chair. The car was abandoned beside the road and sagging badly, as if the springs on one side had been broken. Repeated pounding on the door of the closed store brought no answer. Just as we were about to spread out to look for tracks, fearing Mac had wandered off into the desert, we heard a shout. On the ground, backs to the wall and drunk as skunks, sat Mac, the trader, and the white principal of one of the Hopi day schools with a half-empty gallon jug of wine before them. We soon found out why Mac's car sagged so badly. On the floor behind the driver's seat was a block of petrified wood weighing more than three hundred pounds. Mac had wanted the rock, and the owner, sure no drunk could possibly heft it, had told him it was his. Goodness only knows how Mac got it into the car; it was a miracle he didn't rupture his spleen, or every disk in his spine, in the process.

Mac, of course, wasn't the only one who drove to Winslow to get drunk. In fact, our little crew wore a rut in that road, and while I didn't drink much, I would often go along for the company. Winslow at that time was just barely big enough to have outskirts. There was one main street with stores, bars, and two-foot-high curbs. The high curbs controlled the water that coursed down the streets during cloudbursts and floods from the nearby Little Colorado River. Near the Santa Fe Railroad station was a big, new, luxurious hotel, La Posada, built by Fred Harvey just before the crash of 1929. It was a point of departure for the Fred Harvey Indian Detours into Hopi and Navajo country to the north.

Among the crew in Keams (as it was called), the overall supervisor was Harry Masterson. Since he headed the Indian Emergency Conservation Work (IECW) program at Keams, he outranked MacCurtain. He was slick, ambitious, savvy in the ways of bureaucracies, and spoke in a soft, conspiratorial voice. His wife, a thin, intense woman, lived in Winslow with their two children. She told me once that Masterson sometimes abandoned her and the children without funds or warning. Masterson loved playing the big shot, dressing in polished leather puttees, riding pants, and pressed khaki shirts like a movie actor.

Another notable member of the crew was the mechanic, Jimmy, scion of a wealthy Texas family. He had as massive an alcohol problem as I have ever seen. By his own admission, he was down to a quart a day *on the reservation;* indeed, he stayed there largely because it cut down on his consumption. Jimmy sometimes saw snakes crawling up the sides of his car and through the windows, and under a mild-mannered surface he was one of the most violent human beings I have known. He told me without a trace of emotion of two men who had died at his hand, describing a man's body draped over a barbed wire fence alongside a Texas country road, a man Jimmy shot as he tried to escape. We got along but I never trusted Jimmy, on any level, at any time.

The two engineers were twins named Shockley from Oklahoma, lately with the United States Bureau of Roads. Their wives left an image permanently etched in my memory. At almost any hour of the day, you could find one or the other in a printed cotton sleeveless dress with little or nothing underneath (it was damned hot), leaning over and turning the crank of an ice-cream freezer.

By the end of July the Shockleys had staked out a few dams to be built, but there were no local Indians on the payroll, no work being done, no camps established. We camped in our tents on the edge of Keams Wash and waited for something to happen. I couldn't understand why nobody seemed to care about the job we had been hired to do, which I had learned was to build earthen dams across drainage areas as a way of impounding water for livestock. I was too inexperienced to know that the pattern among the personnel of many government agencies was the unstated assumption that their raison d'être was chiefly the comfort and welfare of their employees.

2

My Navajo Name

PERHAPS THE AGENCY PEOPLE couldn't tolerate my curiosity and energy, for soon after I arrived, I was assigned small jobs that took me out of Keams. They were of little or no consequence but they kept me busy. The first was dynamiting rocks so that Navajo workmen could break them up with sledgehammers to a size easily digested by a rock crusher to make gravel to surface roads. It was my first job as a *boss* over a crew of workmen, and I was glad that my baptism would be with Indians. Somehow it was hard for me to envision myself as straw boss to a bunch of rough-and-tumble, redneck day laborers who settled most arguments with their fists. At the warehouse, where they had everything I needed, no one asked me if I had handled dynamite before. I'm sure they thought I hadn't.

I had learned about dynamite when blasting stumps on my father's place in Missouri years earlier. I knew that dynamite was quite safe if the rules were followed, dangerous if they were not.

It hit me that in a few minutes I was going to have to act like a man and *be* a man—a man accustomed to being in charge. At age nineteen (when I had raised the question of age before I was hired, I was told to say I was twenty-one) I decided I would concentrate only on what I knew. I did not know how to act like a typical roustabout foreman, so I wouldn't even try. Deciding just to be myself and concentrate on the job at hand, I would emphasize the strong card I held, which was that I really did know about dynamite. I had set off charges myself and knew the smell and the feel of fresh dynamite. I also knew the almost brittle character of the fuse, and the shiny thin copper cases of the blasting caps, similiar to a .22 long-rifle casing but open-ended. I always turned the open-ended cap toward the sun so that I could examine the orange mercury fulminate detonating compound two-thirds of the way down the throat of the cap. I was distrustful of caps that were anything but new and shiny, and of dynamite that wasn't slightly moist and a little bit greasy. I would unpack the dynamite myself, separating it from the adjacent sticks and the surrounding sawdust. When beginning with a new box of dynamite, I would first feel the stick, gently squeeze it, and smell it, to be sure it was fresh, that the date on the box was recent, and that all the sticks in the box looked alike. I wanted to make sure that no one had put an old stick in. I knew the familiar feel of the charge as I made a hole with my wooden awl in the end of the stick to receive the cap and the fuse. I knew how soft mud should be in order to hold the charge in place. And I knew I needed to make a clean, fresh diagonal cut on the fuse so that there would be just the right amount of flame from the burning powder to ignite the cap. All these things I knew. What I did not know was the best way to relate to my Indian crew. Except for the one Navajo who had pulled me out of the Steamboat Wash when I was stuck the year before, my only experience with either tribe had been as a tourist. On the other hand, regardless of their feelings or mine, I still had a job to do.

The technical rules for dynamiting were simple, basic, and mandatory: the mercury fulminate caps used to discharge the dynamite had to be kept separate from the dynamite itself. I had seen men put a closed tin box containing caps either in or next to an open box of dynamite—a definite no-no. A slight jarring or a loose tool falling on the caps, and you could be sprouting wings and playing a harp. The caps provide the powerful impact, as well as the flame, to explode the dynamite. Without caps, fresh dynamite—a mixture of nitroglycerin and sawdust—is inert. However, old dynamite is unstable because it crystallizes and in the process becomes hypersensitive. I had heard a story about a man who put a case of outdated dynamite in his car to take it out to the country where it could be destroyed, only to have it go off while he crossed the railroad tracks on the edge of town, leaving behind nothing but a hubcap and a crater.

Naturally, I checked the date on the box as I lifted it onto the truck bed, and I was reassured by the fact that the box had not previously been opened. Looking at the caps, also in a new box, I saw that they had that bright, fresh copper color while the fulminate detonating material was the color of fresh salmon. The fuse was also new and there was plenty of it.

In contrast to dynamite, caps are sensitive to jarring, pinching, or the slightest mechanical deformation. One exploding cap can destroy a hand. Flying copper can put out an eye. With all this in mind, I put the dynamite in the back of the truck and secured the caps in a sling in the cab so that nothing could jar or fall on them while I drove. I was probably being extra cautious about the sling and could have put the caps behind the seat, but I didn't want to take any chances on someone's tossing a heavy iron jack on top of them.

Because fuses burn at a uniform rate, the operator can get to safety. One foot a minute was the standard in my day: eighteen inches, a minute and a half; three feet, three minutes; six feet, six minutes. Like the dynamite, the fuse has to be dry and fresh. Then it should be cut with a razor-sharp knife at just the right angle so that the burning powder train will shoot a jet of flame into the fulminate cap.

The cap must be crimped in precisely the right way—not so tight as to choke off the flame traveling down the hollow core of the fuse on its way to the cap but tight enough to still hold the fuse in place. When I checked out the dynamite that morning, I had asked for a crimping tool. The warehouse clerk had to dig around until he found one, which told me the men handling dynamite on the reservation were not using crimpers. Some men crimped the cap with pliers or even with their teeth! I tried not be around when this happened.

I climbed into my truck and eased out of the agency to a point about three hundred yards past Halderman's store, then turned right toward some house-size boulders where a

Navajo crew was waiting in the shade of piñon pines. I got out of the truck and introduced myself to the one man who came forward and offered me his hand. He was a taciturn man, wearing the garb of working males on the reservation: Levis, blue work shirt, worn brown high-top shoes, and his shiny black hair tied back in a neat bun. He spoke little English. Still, we had little trouble communicating. I didn't have all that much to say and I suppose that by not being chatty, I was communicating that what I had to do was serious business. I was there to dynamite those rocks. My crew was there to break up the rocks with sledgehammers.

I couldn't help but notice how relaxed the Navajos were in the way they walked, talked, and squatted with each other in the shade of the piñons and the rocks. I also noticed that the crew members avoided any eye contact with me, and my initial reaction was that they were hiding something and didn't want to relate to me directly as a man. I soon learned, however, that to give a Navajo a direct look in the eye does not signal sincerity, interest, or man-to-man relating, but anger. My crew's relationship with me was simply detachment. I could live or die, and it wouldn't have made a particle of difference.

In those days Navajos, like all reservation Indians, were legally minors, meaning (among other things) that they couldn't handle dynamite. Therefore, I explained to the man who had greeted me that the crew was not to touch the dynamite under any circumstances. I picked a boulder that seemed to be about the right size for a single stick of dynamite and set about preparing my charge. I asked my interpreter to have one of the men bring me a bucket of mud. Then I fitted the cap to a two-and-a-half-foot fuse, which I inserted in one end of the dynamite. Laying the now-prepared charge on the rock, I packed the mud they had brought me around the charge, patting it down with my hands. The mud was all that was needed because the force of the dynamite blast is not out in all directions but is down. The mud helped to direct the charge downward. Telling the interpreter that the men should take shelter in gullies or behind rocks, I looked at my watch, lit the fuse, and took off myself. Two and a half minutes later, there was the boom of nitroglycerin exploding, leaving only a whiff of blue smoke, the smell of cordite, and a cloud of dust that drifted away to reveal a pile of rocks that moments before had been a large boulder.

I could tell by their smiles and the way they moved that the Navajos enjoyed what was happening. There was the noise, of course, which was impressive, the falling rocks, a large cloud of dust, and eventually the smell of cordite in the air. As soon as the blast went off and the rocks had stopped falling, they jumped up to see the result.

I had passed hurdle number one toward establishing myself in my new role in a new and strange land. The day passed without a hitch. At one point during the second day, I found it necessary to drive back to Keams briefly. I was gone only a few minutes and returned just in time to see my crew scampering to safety behind the boulders in our work area. My heart sank with the realization that I had neglected to remove the blasting caps from the work site when I left, and despite my cautions and explicit orders, the crew had set off a charge on their own. Of course, I well knew that temptation. And matters would have been okay if the charge had gone off, but it hadn't. This was bad. In such cases, either the fuse had been crimped too tightly or not tightly enough so that the traveling flame hadn't reached the mercury fulminate cap.

This was a situation that anyone who has worked with dynamite doesn't even like to think about. A smoldering fuse can set off a blast at any time within hours of the original lighting, and there is no reliable way to tell whether the fuse has really gone out. I realized it would be useless, as well as foolish, to blow my stack at my crew. The act had been done and there was nothing I could do to undo it. Still, a powerful message had been delivered, more penetrating in its effect than anything I could have said. They knew they weren't supposed to set off dynamite on their own. So what could I say? "You bad Indians, you!" I knew they were ashamed. I could see that because they were subdued. So I said nothing and acted as though this was an everyday occurrence that I would handle.

We waited and we waited. Nothing happened. There was dead silence. Nobody said anything (which I later knew was unusual for Navajos). Then after an hour, signaling with my hand for the crew to stay where they were, I crawled toward the dynamite charge on my belly like a soldier in combat. Taking advantage of every bit of cover and approaching the spot the crew had pointed out, I got within six feet and saw the fuse projecting from the mud pie packed around the dynamite on top of a large rock. If the charge went off, I was now too close to escape. Heart in mouth, I edged forward, reached up, and felt for the fuse. I jerked it out and, half turning, tossed it into the arroyo behind me, where the next morning it could be deactivated.

Of course I could simply have left, dismissed the crew, and come back the next morning when I was sure it was safe. But we were within five minutes of Keams, so I would have had to explain my early presence in camp. Everyone would have wanted to know where my crew was and what they were doing. I couldn't bear the thought of the Keams crowd knowing I had allowed this to happen. I would have been the laughingstock of the camp and possibly fired to boot. So I just kept my mouth shut. It had been a close call, but I would never make that mistake again.

I would stand on top of a boulder the size of a small house watching my crew. The heat bordered on the intolerable—110 or 120 degrees Fahrenheit in the shade. If there was any moisture in the air, it didn't show on our crude horsehair hydrometers, which measured zero. Gone was the moderating shield of eastern skies; the clear blue western sky offered little or no screen to the sun's rays. The lay of the land itself intensified the heat. Boulders on top of the barren white-clay earth acted as a camp oven to reflect and radiate heat from all sides. By the time my crew and I had been working together for four days, we had produced a pile of rocks that was in all likelihood enough to satisfy the appetite of the rock crusher for quite a while.

And then something happened that not only impressed me but actually changed my life. For days I had pondered the distance between me and the Navajos. They didn't seem friendly; they were treating me as though they really didn't care what I thought or did. No matter how hard I tried, I could not seem to establish a real relationship with them. But up there on that rock in the blazing heat, I realized that the tide had turned. Perhaps it was because I hadn't blown my stack that second day (white foremen had a habit of blowing their tops in fits of rage, which, I later learned, signaled to the Navajo a loss of control, near psychosis, or an extremely dangerous volatile situation). Maybe it was that we simply went through a scary experience together. Or that I had shown courage. Whatever it was, my interpreter seemed to sense my state of mind. He was more friendly this day—not so impersonal in his greeting—and each man in the crew had said *"Yat-ta-hei"* (pronounced yot-ta-hay as in yacht), the words they use in greeting. I could hardly believe it. I was a person, a human being! We had established contact. We were friends!

From years of observation since then, I have learned that when a Navajo doesn't know you, he has no particular reason to pay attention to you. It is as though you don't exist. But distance and coldness can suddenly be replaced by welcome friendship. In the culture I come from, people pretend that they are very pleased to meet new people, even though they may know nothing about them. When Navajos act pleased to be with you, you can believe them. They must know you first in order for you to become a friend.

The Navajos, in their vast and remote lands, had complete freedom to be themselves without reference to what other people thought. That is, they were inner-directed. It was the human being underneath that was important. When I was with them, I no longer felt the pressure to conform to someone else's idea of who I was supposed to be. For the first time in my life, *I was free to be myself!* At the same time it seemed natural to me, even at that age, to start learning their particular language of behavior, not only to be able to read it correctly but to behave appropriately in their midst.

Supervising the process of making little rocks out of big ones reminded me a bit uneasily of the pictures I had seen of guards and chain gangs working on roads in the South. Smashing rocks was backbreaking work, which was why it was given to prisoners in the South. But here again there was a difference. The Navajos did not treat work as onerous. In fact, they seemed to take pleasure in swinging heavy sledgehammers and watching the rocks splinter into pieces.

One day while the Navajo crew and I were still in the process of getting acquainted, a man from the agency's roads department came out and said that was all the rock they needed for the time being. It was with real regret that I said good-bye to my crew, which they took with equanimity, and I returned to the white folk in the tent village at Keams.

My hiatus was short. My next assignment was working with a Hopi crew. The road up the mesa to Mishongnovi, a Hopi village on the top of Second Mesa, twenty miles west of Keams, had become virtually impassable. My assignment was to fix the worst part of the road next to the sacred Corn Rocks, a prominent pair of tall, thick sandstone pillars. I had seen old photographs of cars and wagons struggling to reach the mesa top via this "road," which was nothing but tracks and grooves made by wagon wheels, weaving in and out of boulders up over rock ledges at impossibly steep inclines.

I knew virtually nothing about the Hopis, but the impressions I had gained from my trip through this area the previous year were powerful. I had felt a deep, inexpressible attraction to the Hopi villages, like nothing I had ever seen or felt before, either in the United States or in Europe. Now, I could feel that the magic was still there.

The Hopis presented themselves as a *peaceful* people, meaning *not warlike, like the Navajos,* and I was soon convinced. My first impression was that they were friendly and open, because many of them spoke English and were easy to talk to. I was three-fourths of the way up the hill to Mishongnovi when I was met by my Hopi crew of fifteen men. They were dressed very much like the Navajo crew except that their black hair was cut like a schoolboy's with bangs in the front and held in place with a headband. They were shorter, somewhat heavier, and not quite so relaxed as the Navajos. I think it was their facial expressions that caught my attention: some were positively handsome and centered, others showed an eagerness to please or to connect, while others were sad or withdrawn. Some gave me little or no feedback. These were mere impressions at first. Yet these impressions seemed to hold up.

I could see that the road hadn't changed much since the time the early photographs had been taken; the ruts were a little deeper, worn in the irregular sandstone and scree that climbed the mesa at an angle barely negotiable by horse-drawn wagons. However, the greatest problem was not the extreme steepness of the grade but the stone steps created by tough rock strata interlarded with softer material. The steps could smash transmissions, radiators, batteries, and oil pans. Yet, since the road next to Corn Rocks at Second Mesa was not to be relocated but simply improved a bit, the job proved to be reasonably straightforward and certainly within my limited experience in road maintenance gained while living on a ranch.

The Indian Emergency Conservation Work (we dropped the *I* except in legal documents and called it ECW) was to provide jobs as well as ways of improving government lands. While the Navajo crew had asked me no questions about the program, my Hopi crew spent most of their time questioning me in detail about how the program was set up, what its purposes were, what part the Hopis would have in deciding where projects would be located, and how the projects would be chosen. Even though I didn't always know the answers to their questions, I was glad to see that the crew seemed genuinely interested.

Since the Hopi crew, unlike the Navajos, were both friendly and loquacious, I felt more at ease from the start. After a few days I was beginning to congratulate myself on how well I was doing with my newfound Hopi friends.

After much discussion and questioning about the work to be done by the ECW, my crew asked me to invite Superintendent Miller to attend a Hopi meeting to be held the next night to discuss the new programs. That day Miller and I were engaged in casual conversation at the side of the road as we looked out across the grand sweep of empty desert south toward the Hopi Buttes and the blue on the distant horizon. The road was really better, and Miller was all smiles. But the moment he heard my question about the Hopi meeting, his face turned red. He went off like a rocket. Calling me every name in the book, he swore to run me off the reservation if he ever heard of my stirring up the Hopis again. He then turned on his heel, strode to his car, slammed the door, and drove off.

After some questioning, I discovered that the crew had expected this response, which was the reason they hadn't asked Miller to the meeting themselves. I had been duped. The entire episode had a surreal quality. I had trouble understanding why Miller thought the Hopis shouldn't discuss the program on their own reservation. Of course it would be difficult dealing with a dozen separate and independent political entities—the Hopi villages. But this was what Collier's program was designed to deal with.

I had obviously been overly romantic about my newfound Hopi "friends." I was beginning to see that nothing is ever simple. Miller's explosion had been too violent simply to have been triggered by one request for a meeting. I learned later that the Hopis would call a meeting about anything at the drop of a hat and had become a thorn in Miller's side, as well as an irritation for some of the other agency people. I had learned an important lesson that Hopi loquaciousness and seeming friendliness could be a mixed blessing, not always to be taken at face value.

It was dawning on me that while I was eager to find acceptance by the people I had been thrust among on the reservation, there were conflicting pressures on me. For example, even such seemingly small matters as how you walked were important. The agency people clearly thought you should stride around like a white man, someone in charge. But I was spending most of my time with the Indians and, because I was fortunate enough to have what the linguists call a high adaptability factor, found myself walking as the Indians do without my being aware of it. Because the walk is an expression of many things, there are ethnic differences in it. Describing a walk, I later learned when I was in the process of developing a notation system, is almost as complex as describing a language.

Most of the people in the government camp were ethnocentric, not really interested in the Indians. But even here there were schisms, notably between those who agreed with John Collier and his programs and those who didn't.

For a young man, because I had no one to back me up— no family, no supportive reservation "establishment," no credentials, no father to whom others would have to answer to if I was not treated right—there were times when it was all quite depressing. I was really alone. But now that the country had become more stabilized after the chaos of the frontier activity, people had settled down and young, free-floating males without backing were not only unusual but fair game for bullies and those who liked to throw their weight around. Realizing all this, I knew that it was essential for me to attach myself to those from whom I could learn.

Then something wonderful happened. One day I went into Slim Halderman's store around the bend from Keams headquarters, and I heard a rustle of whispering among the Navajos who were there. Halderman, a tall, amiable, easygoing man, laughed as I approached.

"You know," he said, "you have a Navajo name now. The Navajos don't address people directly by using their names, so I might as well tell you what your Navajo name is. It's *Chiz Chili,* which means Slim Curly Hair."

I did have curly hair, and I was relieved that they hadn't named me something like Gets Stuck in the Mud or Gets Angry When Frustrated. I figured I had passed my baptism all right. To a Navajo, a person's name is sacred and is endowed with power; they do not abuse that power by calling people by their names to their faces. So my Navajo name was something by which I would eventually be known all over the reservation. It would be a tag for Navajos to attach stories to and would have a history. Because I wouldn't be there long enough, it would not be a big name like Lorenzo Hubbell's Navajo name, *Nakai Tso,* meaning the Fat Mexican. But I never had reason to be ashamed of my name.

I was the first ECW crew member to be named by the Navajos. The name was still with me seven years later when I was doing archaeological surveys over a hundred miles north at Marsh Pass, near Kayenta. I was standing on the platform in front of the old Wetherill trading post with a brand-new, very close-cropped haircut when I heard a passing Navajo on a loping horse sing out, "You-cut-your-hair." He wouldn't call me *Chiz Chili* but wanted me to know he knew my name. His greeting made me feel warm inside, and it told me I was still a friend.

I had an identity.

3

Lorenzo

EVEN A MONTH after my arrival, the Indian Emergency Conservation Work program was still floundering. I knew that people in the commissioner's office back in Washington were bound to get upset. How could they not? Superintendent Miller clearly didn't care, and if our boss, Masterson, was upset about the way things were going, he certainly didn't show it.

In the general idleness of both the agency and the ECW program, there was one exception. The regional headquarters of the Indian Service in Albuquerque had recently assigned a man named Will J. Halloran to the ECW staff. One of the first registered engineers in the state of Arizona (as a state, by the way, Arizona was only some twenty years old), Halloran was tall, rawboned, and quiet-spoken —an outdoor type whose very being communicated competence. I never found out at what level in the Indian Service the decision was made to send in a troubleshooter, but Halloran's arrival at Keams should have been a signal to Miller and his crowd that it was time to stop dragging their feet.

It was soon apparent that Halloran could cut through red tape and get things done. Born in Albuquerque, he had had a lot of mining experience below the border in northern Mexico. In those days, traveling around Sonora and Chihuahua on a horse or a mule—the place was rife with revolutionaries, bandits, and a government unpredictably friendly or hostile to gringos—one learned a lot about survival. He told me that for years he didn't feel safe asleep unless he had a Frontier Colt .45 tucked between his shoulder blades with his elbows above his head and both his hands on the butt of the gun. The slightest disturbance would bring him upright like a jack-in-the-box, gun cocked, aimed and ready.

Halloran immediately set about resurveying the road to Pinyon, and over Keeley's opposition he started hiring Indians and actually managed to get a few on the payroll. Equipment began to move out to the road, and you didn't have to be clairvoyant to see that it was only a matter of time before roadwork would begin in earnest. But, in the ECW tents, still nothing was happening.

Then a man named Jay Nash paid the agency a visit. A former professor at New York University, Nash was a trusted deputy of John Collier, the commissioner. Customarily, when someone from Washington arrived on the reservation, Miller and his people would enact an obsequious ritual. Miller would wait outside the office building, smiling and bowing, accompanied by Keeley, who would try to look pleasant for a change. The bigwig would be ushered into Miller's office, coffee would be served, and polite inquiries would be made about the trip out and the commissioner's health, along with a few casual remarks about things being a bit slow getting started—all a smoke screen. The assumption was that apart from budgetary matters and policy guided by politics, Washington couldn't possibly be interested in programs on the ground. After the bigwig's departure, everything would settle back into the familiar lethargic rut.

But as it turned out, Jay Nash's visit was specifically about programs on the ground. He spoke as if the words were coming out of the commissioner's mouth and he had been sent to get things going. Instead of sitting through the ritual greeting and pleasantries, Nash peremptorily got rid of Miller, saying that he wanted to talk to someone on the ECW staff. When he arrived at the tent area, ignoring my superiors, he strode directly toward me like a hawk diving on a mole. He took me by the elbow and asked if there was a place we could talk. There were several explanations of why he picked me and not someone else. The most logical was that I was the only one present who had been hired directly out of Collier's office, who could be counted on to be sympathetic to his new policies. Nevertheless, I was somewhat stunned. Not knowing what he could possibly have in mind, I suggested the shade of the cottonwoods nearby for our conversation.

Nash questioned me at length about why there were no camps yet and who was holding things up. I told him that nothing was happening and there seemed to be some covert resistance to the whole idea of Collier's new program, though I didn't know the source of this resistance. I didn't say that I thought the problem lay with Miller and Keeley. I told him of a notion among the agency staff that Hopis and Navajos would kill each other if they were put in a camp together. That idea, I told him, struck me as preposterous, perhaps merely a ruse. And I told him that given my standing at the low end of the totem pole, I wasn't in the best position to take corrective action. That made Nash angry.

"Goddamn it," he blurted out, "I don't care if you have to carry those tents out on your back and build that camp yourself. Collier wants camps and he is going to have camps! And I want a camp in a week. Do you understand that?"

Thunderstruck, I said, "Yes, sir." Fifteen minutes later Nash was just a memory and on his way to Tuba City.

And that was that. Nash, just by his actions, redefined my relationship with everyone in the Keams Canyon hierarchy. He had in effect ordered me to ignore the chain of command and play an active roll in the administrative process and get the show on the road. Pondering my newly defined situation, I found myself wondering what Halloran would do in such a circumstance. I decided he sure as hell wouldn't expect the bureaucrats in the agency to straighten things out, and my own intuition was saying loudly, "Stay away from Miller. All you'll get for your trouble is another bawling out." So I asked myself who might have some idea of what was going on, what the obstacles were, and how to get past them. It struck me that if anyone would know, it was Lorenzo Hubbell. Despite Miller's injunction to stay away from traders, I got in my car and made the thirty-two-mile trip to Oraibi.

About an hour or more later, I was sitting in Lorenzo's

office with Navajos, relatives who were working for him, and a couple of government people from outside our agency, all waiting for a turn to talk to Lorenzo Hubbell.

About fifty years old at the time, Lorenzo was a large man with stained teeth, several of which were missing. He chewed tobacco, which he spat into a coffee can on the floor next to his right foot. It seemed that he would use this interruption whenever he needed time to think. Tremendous in girth, he had mottled skin (perhaps the result of a liver disorder, I thought), and he spoke in a thick, raspy whisper. While the expression on his face didn't reveal much, there was an amused twinkle, which would come and go in his eyes like sunlight when windblown clouds scud between the earth and the sun. And the twinkle became a glint when it seemed that people weren't being straight with him. Like all businessmen in the West in those days, he wore the pants of a gray suit held up by narrow suspenders, a white shirt with narrow stripes, and a straight-brimmed Stetson. Because of his girth, his pants had two pockets on each side, one in front of the side seam and one on the other side. I had never noticed such an arrangement before but understood immediately how it had happened. I realized that the pockets in men's pants are designed in relation to the side, or outermost, seam. Normally that positions the rear pocket so that it is just around the corner, as it were, from the front pocket. However, if the tailor is dealing with about fifteen inches of cloth on each side of the middle back seam, the so-called back pocket ends up just to the side of the front pocket. So what you get is two side pockets, one beside the other.

Then I realized that it was my turn to talk with Lorenzo. Taking a deep breath and bracing myself, I forgot the difference in our age and status and told him as clearly as possible about Nash's visit to Keams, which had left no doubt that Collier wanted camps and was determined that we get them going. At the mention of Collier's name, Lorenzo led me out of his office and into his bedroom next door. As the conversation lengthened, he took me into the kitchen. And when it came to the issue of what the camps would do for (or to) traders, we went outside and talked leaning against the adobe wall of the building. This, I discovered, was a typical pattern: each place was for a different degree of confidentiality, from the open forum of the office to the complete privacy of the outdoors.

Lorenzo wanted to know what the camps were supposed to do. He asked how many there would be and for how long. I explained the realities of the situation—namely, that as long as there was a road to be built, the camps made sense because we could haul the men to work in trucks. But how long could the roadwork last? The ECW plan called for a twenty-five-mile stretch of nine-foot-crown truck trail. With Halloran on the job, it certainly would not take very long. Furthermore, as soon as the road was finished, there was no other planned construction project on the reservation—building dams or developing springs—that would require enough men in one place to warrant even one camp. Nevertheless, Collier wanted camps on this reservation, and I had been told by Nash to see to it that they were built. I wondered why the commissioner was so set on camps. I gathered that they were part of his program for all reservations; otherwise, there wouldn't have been a special category of jobs designated for "camp managers." By then I had come to the conclusion that the bureaucrats in Keams were resisting the camps and, furthermore, that it was the lack of camps that was holding up all the rest of the ECW work. I told Lorenzo about the idiotic notion advanced as an excuse for inaction—that the Indians wouldn't go into the camps because the rivalry between the Navajos and the Hopis might lead to violence and bloodshed. Lorenzo dismissed this rationalization as pure nonsense.

Gradually I began to sense what might lie behind all his questions about camps. *The traders didn't want them.* Why? Because they feared that the money spent building the camps and feeding the Indians would not end up in the Indians' pockets and would therefore bypass the traders' tills, which were badly in need of replenishing. This fear was justified and I did not understand it myself at first, simply because I didn't know enough about the trading business as it was run in those days. It was evident, however, that no one in the government had thought to explain Collier's plan to Lorenzo or any other trader the way I had just done. Standing in the hot sun outside his kitchen door, Lorenzo told me in his gravelly voice to let him know when I wanted Indians for the camps and he would see to it that I had them.

The effect of my short visit to Oraibi was like pulling a key log out of a log jam. From that point on, things happened fast. Carpenters appeared and went to work, supplies moved, bids for food and supplies were let. It was like magic. Even though it was happening in front of my very eyes, it was difficult to believe that for once there was action after all the stalling and foot-dragging. Within a week we had a camp: tents, a screened-in mess tent, cookstoves, storage areas, latrines, and even athletic equipment. I was amazed.

A tiny crumb of an idea came to me that something like the old Hopi schism of Friendlies and Hostiles was going on among the permanent whites on the reservation, except that one faction was the government higher-ups and the traders, and the other faction was Collier's New Deal men. It was just an intuition, and apart from Lorenzo and Miller, I had no clue to who the players were, the kind of game it was, or the rules by which they were playing. It seemed that the government at the local level—possibly even in cahoots with the traders—had taken on the role of the hostiles (to Collier and to progress), while the New Deal represented the friendlies' position.

One thing was certain, however, in the slippery and shadowy world of the bureaucracy: Lorenzo Hubbell wielded an enormous influence among both Indians and whites on the Hopi and Navajo reservations. He was a man I wanted to know better, and luckily, that is just what happened.

At the turn of the century, Lorenzo (only nineteen years old—about the age I was when we met) had just taken over the Keams Canyon trading post. His father, the famous J. L. Hubbell, had bought the post for Lorenzo to run. It was his first and marked the beginning of what would later be an extensive chain of stores. This one had been founded in 1869, on the heels of the Civil War, by Thomas Keam, an Englishman.

Thirty years later the now-mature Lorenzo would talk about the Keams experience with such clarity, it seemed as if the events had occurred only yesterday. His first partner, informal mentor, and close friend was Ed Thacker, an older man who had married a Navajo woman. The couple had one child, a girl. Lorenzo's relationship with Ed Thacker was more akin to that of older and younger brothers than simply partners in a business enterprise. Such a relationship would have been fostered by the older Hubbell, placing his son under the wing of a trusted and experienced trader to keep him company, help out with the practical matters of running a trading post, and be there to back him up in moments of crisis, which were certain to occur.

These were still dangerous times. In 1910 the trader Richard Wetherill was ambushed outside his trading post at Pueblo Bonito and killed by Navajos thought to have been incited to violence by the Indian agent. The Indian agents, for the most part, isolated themselves from the Indians in time, in space, and by administrative fiat. The agents hated the traders and yet each depended on the other for survival. This has never been satisfactorily analyzed; perhaps it was out of envy, perhaps it was because the agents couldn't totally control the traders. The agents' link was to Washington, the traders' to the Indians. Agents were appointed bureaucrats, and the traders were entrepreneurs on the reservation by choice. Indian agents (and missionaries) did their best to deprive the Indians of their religion and their culture and never hesitated to tell the Indians that they and their way of life were inferior. Lorenzo and other traders were the only white men who did not play an active role in the massive effort to brainwash the Indians, and they paid a price.

Particularly vivid were Lorenzo's recollections of the petty harassment he received at the hands of Superintendent Lemmon during his brief term of office in Keams. From the day he set foot on the reservation, Lemmon—who fit the archetype of Herman Wouk's Captain Queeg in *The Caine Mutiny*—made it quite clear that he was out to get Lorenzo. That Lorenzo was young, Spanish, and had a partner married to a Navajo woman (in the days of prejudice against "squaw men") may have had something to do with it. That Lorenzo was the scion of a rich and powerful territorial family undoubtedly made him an even more appetizing target.

Lemmon was the seventh disaster in human form, representing the United States Government, to descend on the Hopis between the years 1889 and 1904. The policies of kidnapping children and sending them away to the white man's schools, imprisoning Hopi leaders at Alcatraz, forcing the allotment of lands, and disrupting ceremonial life were indignities that all six of the superintendents of that period happily carried out. Lemmon was no different from his predecessors, except that he may have been a somewhat less competent administrator, as his botched attempt to force the Hopi protesters out of their kivas attests.

Lemmon showed absolutely no concern for his obligation to pay the Indians what he owed them or appreciation of what Lorenzo had done by way of calming the Navajos. According to Lorenzo, he simply grew even more venomous, vindictive, and picayune in his behavior toward the young trader. Lorenzo kept wondering: "What next?"

Then, something did happen. Late one night after he and Ed Thacker had closed the store and were eating dinner, there was a loud pounding on the door. "Open up in there!" a voice shouted. "Mr. Lemmon says to open up!" They opened the door and Lemmon's clerk thrust a note at them: "Hubbell, come to the agency at once. Signed Lemmon." Lorenzo told the clerk he had to saddle a horse and would be right up. Noting that Lemmon had been acting so maniacally, they thought he might even shoot Lorenzo, so both men saddled up. Thacker took along his carbine, and as they approached the agency headquarters, he trailed behind so that Lorenzo seemed alone. Entering the squat building that housed Lemmon's office, Lorenzo was greeted by a Lemmon he had never seen before.

His open hands were outstretched. In a voice dripping with honey, Lemmon said, "Mr. Hubbell, do come in. Please be seated. So kind of you to come out on a dark night like this. I asked you to come at night because I didn't want anyone to hear our conversation." Words tumbled out of the man's trembling mouth. "Mr. Hubbell, I'm in terrible trouble. The whole agency is in trouble and I don't know what to do, or what they will do to me when they find out."

Warily, Lorenzo listened to Lemmon's story. Through mismanagement or God knows what tomfoolery, Lemmon had managed to expend the entire annual budget of the agency in less than six months. The agency was broke. There were no funds—no salaries for the schoolteachers or the clerks, no money to run the dormitories, pay the cooks, or buy food for the schoolchildren. As far as Lorenzo was concerned, there was only one thing to do. In the Hubbell tradition, he underwrote the entire operation for the rest of the year. I assume he didn't pay Lemmon's salary, but it is not impossible. He never told me how or if he was repaid. I knew that the government made no provision for eventualities of this sort. Later, reading the Hopi artist Fred Kabotie's book, I also learned of an event Lorenzo never mentioned to me: the time he fed an entire group of Hopis who, following a factional dispute, were starving after being expelled by the government from Hotevilla, where they had taken refuge.

In 1905 J. L. Hubbell bought another store, this time in Oraibi, from F. W. Voltz, a trader who ran three posts between Oraibi and Winslow. Thirteen years later Lorenzo left Keams and moved into the Oraibi store. By that time the family empire of trading posts under Lorenzo's aegis extended from Ganado in the east, to Oraibi in the west, to

Winslow in the south, and to Black Mountain in the north. Lorenzo was far from an ordinary Indian trader. By the time we first met in 1932, he had become a world figure. His reputation had filtered into the nooks and crannies inhabited by the European intelligentsia and had spread to Australia and New Zealand, as well as to Washington. It seemed strange at first that a single man, in such modest surroundings, would be so well known. Today it would be impossible because only public figures whose fame has been spread by the media are known as Lorenzo was then.

Several factors were at work that contributed to Lorenzo's fame. First, the world was smaller then (the population of the globe has more than doubled). Those who traveled were fewer and more likely to know each other. There was already a base of fame and contacts in high places when Lorenzo started trading at Keams. And there was his famous father, about whom books had been written, a friend of presidents and confidant of Theodore Roosevelt. Lorenzo's uncle on his mother's side was reputed to be the largest sheep man in the world. That is, the Hubbell name then was even more famous than it is now. There was no place for travelers to stay on the reservation, so Lorenzo lodged them and fed them at his kitchen table, and they listened to him talk about the Indians. No one knew as much as he did. And while his reputation was different from and not so wide as his father's, there can be no doubt that his own charismatic presence contributed greatly to Lorenzo's fame.

Though Lorenzo was a Republican and the Administration was Democratic, Secretary of Agriculture Henry Wallace looked to him for advice on agricultural policy for the nation. John Collier was a frequent visitor and, before he was commissioner of Indian Affairs, a frequent consultant.

Secretary of the Interior Harold Ickes also kept in touch on a regular basis through his wife, who made periodic visits to Oraibi and sat at our table along with the usual crowd of foreign visitors, Lorenzo's truck drivers, and whoever else happened to be stopping there for the night.

There was always a hidden air of contradiction about Lorenzo. He lived modestly, yet the cash flow for his business ran into six figures and more. A more ostentatious man would have built himself a business complex, reflecting his power, influence, and substantial worth. But Lorenzo intuitively chose to live in such a way that no one, regardless of status or ethnicity, would stay away. The Oraibi trading post and the attached, somewhat dilapidated, unpretentious living quarters—two rooms, a kitchen, and a porch—were arranged so that anyone would enter. Yet this meager setup at times accommodated up to a dozen guests of both sexes. The men slept on the porch rolled up in quilts, which a moment before had rested on the top shelves of the store; the women slept in the two inside bedrooms. The key to the privy hung on a nail by the kitchen door. The kitchen was cramped, but intimate. It housed a large, old-style wood range, a refrigerator, a china cabinet, a sink, and a large oval table. When I was working in the area, this modest establishment would become my home and the place where I met people of importance and interest; most important, it became my personal forum, conducted under Lorenzo's experienced eye. It was here I learned to accept cultures other than my own as true cultures.

Lorenzo was accustomed to making trips, lasting anywhere from a week to three months. He never announced his departures in advance or said where he was going or how long he would be gone. People talked about the time he was gone for six months without a word to a soul, reappearing one day as though he had dropped out of the sky.

He was able to take off on these mysterious journeys because of a man named Fletcher Corrigan. Fletch was a relative of the Wetherills, an ex-marine corporal, later buried in Kayenta. As a young man—following World War I—he had *walked* the eighty miles from Winslow to Oraibi, turning up on Lorenzo's doorstep looking for a job. I kept asking myself, "How the hell could that man walk eighty miles across the desert on the mere chance of getting a job?"

Fletcher Corrigan was big—six feet five or six inches, at least—broad of shoulder, muscular with a tiny butt and a beer belly, which hung over and partially hid a belt pushed down to his hips by the mass above.

Occasionally one encounters individuals who are out of place. Such folk are like an atomic particle knocked free from the binding forces of the nucleus of an atom. Once free, they never seem to be able to get back to their own niche and either settle in some incongruous environment or roam the globe like restless gypsies. Fletch was one of the former. His proper ambience was a Dublin pub; the greatest contradiction lay in his being on the reservation at all. As a species, human beings are extraordinarily adaptable, possibly one of the most adaptable on the face of the earth. To make life bearable, Fletch adapted. The day-to-day management of the Hubbell enterprises rested on two sets of shoulders, Lorenzo's and Fletch's. Both knew what they were doing, but things seldom went smoothly between them. They fought like two Plains Indian braves galloping parallel to each other on horseback, launching barbs at every opportunity in a daily running battle.

Lorenzo sat at a desk that was between the only window in the room and the stairwell, which led into the store on his right. Fletch was hunched over a minuscule shelf that performed as a desk. Above his head was a single light and the store's multiple account books neatly stacked on a narrow shelf. When strangers were not present, the eight-foot space separating the two men was alive with invectives and the palpable current of impatience on Lorenzo's part, and envy and even hatred on Fletch's. When guests—visitors or dignitaries—were present, Lorenzo would hold forth and Fletch would sit there in silence, listening, hunched over his account books, a tight bundle of passion, just barely able to contain himself.

While working for Lorenzo, Fletch had met, courted, and married Isabel, the beautiful olive-skinned, black-haired daughter of Lorenzo's partner, Ed Thacker. Isabel's Navajo mother was a woman of great style, character, and strength, and Isabel was their only child. When Ed Thacker had a heart attack while dipping sheep, his deathbed wish was that Lorenzo would always look after his "little girl." Lorenzo always did. After she married Fletch, the couple moved away for a while, but soon they were back and living in a modern, comfortable house Lorenzo had built for them a couple of hundred yards north of the store. Lorenzo's quarters had one cold-water tap and an outhouse, but the Corrigans enjoyed a modern kitchen and bath.

The anthropologist Mischa Titiev, who was studying the Hopis at the time, used to visit the Corrigans where one could get a hot bath, a welcome change from fieldwork in Old Oraibi. For people visiting Oraibi who obviously couldn't take the camping Lorenzo provided at the store, the Corrigans' house could be counted on as a comfortable, middle-class haven.

The challenge of the country, particularly of getting stuck, was formidable to everyone but Fletch. Once when we were swapping tales of getting stuck, he capped them all with a combination of pride and amusement, as well as a trace of nostalgia, when he told how one of his Buicks had been stuck in the Oraibi Wash. He was digging out the Buick's narrow, high tires that were sunk into the sandy bottom when the floodwaters hit. When the wash subsided a day later, only the top of the car was visible, a black rectangle in the middle of the moist, sandy bottom. Most people would have left the car there; everyone knew that sand and mud would have penetrated to the most inaccessible places in the engine and power train. But with Irish stubbornness, Fletch hired two Hopis with a team and exhumed the car, leaving a hole the size of a small house in the sand. Somehow they managed to get that sand-filled hulk on skids, although it must have weighed tons. Days later the carcass, oozing mud, graced the smooth clay ground next to the porch on the south side of the store, where it was protected from the wind. Bit by bit the Buick was disassembled; the parts were spread out to dry on hides and canvas staked to the ground. Water and sand had penetrated the motor, the wheels, the brakes, the transmission and clutch and had pushed past the protective grease seals, even into the rear end. Finally, all the parts were there, each in its place like an exploded drawing in a maintenance manual: valves, valve springs, valve guides, rocker arms, bushings, bearings, camshaft, timing gears, pistons, piston rings, crankshaft, connecting rods, and wrist pins. Every part was laboriously cleaned, oiled, reassembled. The parts that couldn't be cleaned, like the instruments on the dashboard, were replaced. Even the upholstery was cleaned or replaced. This monumental and painstaking task kept Fletch occupied for an entire fall and winter. By spring the work was finished. A new battery replaced the old one, oil was put in the crankcase and gas in the gas tank. Would the starter and bendix work? Was the timing correct? Would the fuel pump function? All were checked and seemed to be in order. The carburetor was primed, ignition on, starter engaged—cough, cough, pop-pop, wheeze, wheeze—and finally, just when they were about to give up, purr-purr, the rhythmic sound of a perfectly functioning engine. No wonder Fletch was proud.

Isabel and Fletch's father, a slight old man of mild disposition, were the two satellites that revolved around the heavier mass of Fletch's personality, giving him assurance that he was somebody. Old Mr. Corrigan ran the post office attached to Lorenzo's store. Isabel ran the home and played hostess to Lorenzo's guests and Fletch's friends. On the occasions when Lorenzo departed without notice and with no word about where he was going or how long he would be gone, the store would settle into a monotonous routine. Fletch kept his post, like a regimental CQ on duty in an orderly room at night. The squabbling and torment were gone, but so was the life. In a state of suspended animation, one day would be pretty much like the next. Nothing happened. When Lorenzo reappeared, just as suddenly as he had left, our small world would begin to throb and vibrate again, reconnected to its own vital force. It wasn't that Lorenzo ran the store—the store took care of itself—but the center of the Hubbell universe was now reestablished. Fletch, like a regimental sergeant major when the colonel has just walked in, not only was restricted again to his own smaller orbit of influence but was jounced and bounced around by the unpredictable perturbations of Lorenzo's larger mass.

4

The Experience
of Place

THROUGH WHATEVER MAGIC conjured up by Lorenzo Hubbell, John Collier had his first camp within a
week. It was situated on a wide and gentle slope fifty feet
or so in elevation above the sandy floor of the Wepo Wash,
twelve to fifteen miles north of the Hopi villages of Walpi,
Sichomovi, and Hano. When I think of these villages, I see
them in my mind's eye as a floating island suspended in air
high above the desert landscape below. I am not sure of the
exact meaning of this image except that it is true. Somehow the presence of the villages on the mesa top had al-
tered the relationship of mesa to village, transforming

what had once been separate entities into a single coherent whole.

A ridge running northeast, dividing the Wepo and Oraibi drainages, connected the Hopi village of Shongopavi to Pinyon, making it the natural location for a road to Pinyon, which until then had been one of the most isolated spots in the country. The ridge itself was characterized by a series of ledges of outcropping sandstone with a cover of piñons, juniper trees, sagebrush, and open islands of grassland. One of these open spots, next to a windmill storage tank and small pond where stock could quench their thirst, was selected as the site for our camp. The trees were a source of wood for Second Mesa villages, and a long spur of desert grassland projecting north from the Hopi villages into the heart of Navajo country provided forage for sheep.

While there was nothing particularly dramatic or even noticeably unusual about the setting, the locale turned out to be one of the most inherently tranquil places I have ever known. I will never know if my feelings were a reaction to the preceding discomfort and confusion at Keams or were induced by the place itself. (There are places like that.) For the first time since I arrived on the reservation, I could feel the stress of the politicking and psychological undercurrents of Keams begin to slough away. Here I was at ease with myself and at one with nature. There were about fifty Indians—Navajos and Hopis—in camp along with Mac-Curtain, Halloran and his wife, and me. Mac could have stayed in Keams, but instead he showed up with his gear, moved in, and made himself at home. The predictable camp routine—and the place—satisfied his soul in a way Keams could not and temporarily freed him of his need for alcohol. An essence emanated from the earth, the vegetation, and the sky above, which had a calming effect on the nerves—an essence impossible to assign to any of the senses. Nevertheless, in my time on the reservation, I discovered such places again and again and found that all the Indians knew about them. They thought of them as *power places.*

The Indians—the Navajos in particular—were in an upbeat mood: laughing, carousing, joking, pushing each other playfully like a bunch of kids. I reveled in my own peace of mind; life in general was as it should be. Nevertheless, I found it hard to believe that life could be so simple. I had a niggling feeling at the back of my mind that we were living in an artificial world of our own making. I saw the camp as a transition in time and place, a sort of antechamber to the reality that lay before me.

The Indians were happy to have work for which they were well paid, jobs that gave them much-needed cash on which to live as well as money to repay debts to the traders. The work kept them occupied and gave them companionship (which was deeply important to the Navajos, who spent much of their lives in small family groups), adequate shelter, and—equally important—an inexhaustible supply of food prepared by our two Hopi cooks, Cecil and Arthur. We brought in ingredients from the railroad towns of Winslow and Holbrook, ninety miles south. Breakfast was ham and eggs, mutton, panfried potatoes, toast, butter and jam. Most of the men would eat two servings, some three. It was clear many of the Navajos could hardly remember what it was like to have a full stomach. Even after sixty-one years, the memory of our mess tent still fills my heart with warmth. The men, back from work on the road, poured in cheerfully, pushing and shoving in their eagerness to get at the food. They would sit down to eat crowded together cheek by jowl, Navajos and Hopis inter-mingled like a bunch of English public school boys excited, impatient, hungry, and happy because there was enough for everyone. One thin old Navajo, fork in hand, would put one knee on the table, heft himself up, and leaning forward, spear a large slice of mutton from a dish in the center.

Although the Hopis and the Navajos at Camp #1 did not end up killing each other, as had been predicted, I began to see the differences between the two tribes right from the start. Their music was one example. It was the season (late summer) of the Hopi Butterfly Dance, and each evening the Hopis would gather together and practice their songs, which were slow, rhythmic, and earthy, almost like relics from the ancestors' underworld. The Butterfly Dance songs had an organic quality, like bees in a hive. By contrast, the Navajo falsetto-voiced Yeibichai songs were robust, intense, and penetrating.

Depending on the topography and the wind, a single Navajo singing on horseback could be heard a mile to a mile and a half away. Here at our camp twenty Navajos in a huddle would split the night with the magic of their voices. In the daytime, during work, the two groups tended to keep to their own company. Sometimes at night I would see the Hopis, Coleman lamp in hand, track a rattlesnake whose spoor they had detected in the vicinity of the tents. The first time I saw them I wondered what they were do-ing. Several men would be clustered together in the evening blackness with their bent-over figures sharply outlined by the single bright light of the lamp. Out of curiosity, I joined them and, discovering that they were tracking a rattle-snake, followed them in a wide loop, which ended in a tent full of lumber. There was the snake all right, large as life and twice as threatening, rattling away with the sound no one who has ever heard it forgets. I wanted to know if they were looking for snakes for the Snake Dance. "No. We killem." Why? "We don't like snakes. Snakes bite and maybe you will die." It appeared that except for the Snake Priests, the Hopis like everyone else were afraid of rattlers.

While the Hopis were quick to interact with white people, the Navajos were more reserved. At least some of these distinctions could be traced to differences in familiarity with, and use of, the English language. Many more Hopis than Navajos could speak English then. For realistic purposes, one had to operate on the assumption that none of the Navajos would be able to speak English. With this in mind, one could observe a lot without depending on language. Taken as a whole, the Navajos were the more playful of the two, the more ebullient and joyful in interacting with each other. Clearly these were not the only differences, but just the ones I observed at the time.

Windmills on the reservation were like water holes in the game parks in Kenya: practically everything that moves comes to a water hole created by the overflow from a storage tank. In the morning I would go down and look for the tracks of small mammals as well as larger ones up to and including coyotes and bobcats. I would not have been surprised to see a mountain lion, but I don't remember any. All the sheep in the area came at least once a day, driven by their Navajo shepherds—women in long skirts and velveteen blouses, aided by sheepdogs who could scarcely control the thirsty herd when they smelled the water. Sometimes two impatient herds would become mingled. When this happened, the two shepherds—cursing profusely in Navajo—would have to hike up their skirts and wade into the water to carry their sheep out one by one to a location where the sheepdog could keep them together. (Cecil, our Hopi cook, told me that the pale yellow of the women's inner thighs was exciting to him and that he never tired of watching the Navajo shepherds hike up their skirts.) A few of the shepherd women would pretend that they were trying to hold their sheep back, but let them run forward on the chance that in the sorting-out process the shepherd could pick up one or two lambs from the other herd.

One day while I was watching the never-ending chain of events at the pond, a whirlwind descended to earth, kicking up a swirl of dust around one of the Navajo workmen. Being buffeted by wind-borne sand looked plenty uncomfortable, but the man was terrified. To the Navajo, the whirlwind was *chindi*—full of evil that can make you sick, almost as bad as being bewitched. While I didn't think that I would be bewitched, I learned to avoid being caught in whirlwinds, particularly if they are going counterclockwise. According to the Navajos, the counterclockwise whirlwinds are the really bad ones. I began to learn that many things in Navajo life were *chindi*. A home in which someone died was *chindi,* and to avoid having to move out of a perfectly good home, Navajos would take relatives near death and place them beside the road in the hope that some passing white man would take them to the hospital. Part of the Navajo fear of hospitals in those days was that people died in them. There were other places that were *chindi;* one was an outcropping of rock called a hogback along the spine of Black Mesa, and I took to hurrying past it when some mission took me that way.

In my experience, each country has a flavor all its own, a mystique unique to it and its people. This flavor, or "feel," is independent of topography, flora and fauna, temperature, climate, or even smells. It springs from the old nature spirits, gods, ghosts, witches, and demons, which are a vital part of most peoples' worlds. White Americans have very few spirits, so their country is by comparison apt to feel empty and barren based on this supersensory scale. The flavor of Hopi and Navajo country was almost palpable, and I began to catalog mentally the places I visited in terms of the feelings they evoked. I was discovering a new kind of geography.

Just as people have characteristics that differentiate them from each other, the Hopi villages were different in the sensations they released in me—sensations that were most pronounced at Walpi and Old Oraibi. Walpi was a multi-storied pueblo packed on a narrow and precipitous spur of First Mesa, separated from the other First Mesa villages Sichomovi and Hano by a twenty-foot-wide vertical-sided strip. In its brooding isolation, Walpi had a powerful spiritual, totally alien quality. There was nothing threatening about these (for lack of a better word) spirits; they were just foreign to me. I was recently reminded of my reaction to Walpi when I arranged for three Australian Aborigines to visit the Hopi and Navajo country. When they approached the narrow strip separating Walpi and Sichomovi, all three stopped as though they had run into an invisible wall. They said they felt a powerful spiritual presence there that was alien to them, and they did not want to become involved with such forces unless they were properly prepared.

Old Oraibi—the most ancient of all settlements in the United States—exuded an aura of suffering, pain, suspicion, even hostility. Even though Old Oraibi was visible on the mesa top above Lorenzo's store, I spent little time there and never felt quite comfortable in that vicinity. There was too much pain and agony there, too many witches (called, in Hopi, *two hearts*). The village had been there too long and had seen too many feuds and altercations. It was dying.

There were many positive places. When I had to drive from Camp #1 to Keams, I took a shortcut that saved twenty-five miles and an hour; it was a twelve-mile stretch of road, which was one of my favorites on the reservation. With a view of the peach orchards on the mesa top north of Hano, the stretch along Wepo Wash was pervaded by an aura of entwining mystery and tranquillity. The road ran through, around, and over sand dunes, down the banks of the wash that started the steep, winding climb to a notch in the mesa. It was originally a trail for goats and donkeys, and its switchbacks had been lengthened just enough to accommodate vehicles. Even in the best of times it was difficult to negotiate, but when it was wet, there was only one viable direction: down. The road was banked toward the mesa, keeping wheeled vehicles from slipping over the edge, and you could shift into low gear and simply slide down like a toboggan.

Another kind of experience of place on the reservation is summed up in the word *hashklish*. It is the onomatopoeic Navajo word for mud. There was absolutely no stigma attached to getting stuck in *hashklish* for the simple reason that everyone did, regardless of driving skill. You negotiated a mudhole by stepping on the gas and maintaining momentum—just a hair below takeoff speed. You slipped and slid, yawed, bounced, and prayed (we all prayed in our own way to our own gods) that the mud in the ruts wouldn't be deep enough to hang up the car on the high center. But as often as not there would be a sudden decrease in speed followed by that helpless feeling when the wheels spun freely and all traction was lost. In winter, driving to Winslow meant eighty miles of slush and slime, with chains *and* rope wrapped around all four wheels. Simply to drive on Winslow's hard pavement was one of the greatest luxuries of my life. Once, because my work was nearby, I spent an entire week floundering in the mud —getting stuck, digging out, getting stuck again. I should have waited for the ground to dry, as everyone else did.

In Camp #1, I spent a lot of time with Halloran, who taught me that if you worked *with* instead of against nature, things simply went better. Storing water aboveground by building dams, for example, wastes huge quantities of valuable water through evaporation and seepage, especially in the West, where the dry air soaks up water like a sponge. Halloran developed a system for driving the floodwaters in arroyos underground where the water would be kept until needed. He made what are called basket dams— stone sausages wrapped in hog wire laid at intervals along the bed of an arroyo. These porous structures slowed the floodwater just enough to drive a portion of the floodwater down into the sandy subsoil underlying the arroyo bed. At some convenient or relevant point, all that was necessary to bring the underground stream to the surface was to sink a narrow trench down to bedrock across the valley and fill it with concrete. All of which could be done at a laughably low cost, without disfiguring the land and with little loss of water. Unfortunately, special interests and the need to conquer nature often win out over such commonsense schemes as Halloran's. In our country, the beaverlike approach of the Army Corps of Engineers and the Bureau of Land Reclamation has dictated that dams are a solution to everything, when there are many places where the solution to the need for water is simpler, cheaper, less disfiguring to the landscape, and more efficient.

The time I spent at Camp #1 on the reservation was in many ways the most secure and least stressful. The camp was so successful that I was told to move to Pinyon, where Camp #2 was being built at the northern end of the road our crews were working on. Taking Arthur, one of the cooks, with me, I set out for Pinyon. We were there all of one day and a night when a Navajo rode up on horseback with a note telling me to drop everything and go to the trading post a little over a mile east, on the other side of the headwaters of the Oraibi Wash, run by Lorenzo's cousin, George. When I arrived, I was greeted by George, a short, red-faced, round man, even fatter than Lorenzo. George was never one to beat around the bush. "The road-work has stopped," he said. "Halloran has been fired, and the camps have been closed. You're to pack up your gear and return to Keams. I just got it on the telephone."

He said that Halloran, using road graders with blades eighteen feet long, had found it more feasible to build an eighteen-foot-crown road than to adhere to the nine-foot specifications that defined a truck trail, which was what we were supposed to be building. The regulations dictated that roads with crowns of more than nine feet were not the responsibility of our ECW program but of the Bureau of Roads! Score one more for the bureaucracy. We repacked our things and returned to Camp #1, where I said good-bye to Halloran and his wife. I told them I would miss them, and I have ever since.

I assumed that my days were numbered as well. None of the other work the ECW was to do required camps or someone to run them. I was utterly surprised when the ECW boss, Masterson, told me that I would be working out of Oraibi as a group foreman building earth dams. I would be a neighbor of Lorenzo Hubbell's for a time, and in the core of the Hopi lands.

5

The Hopis

ONCE ENSCONCED in Oraibi in a dark little house with a peaked roof, an outdoor privy, and no running water or lights, I returned to Keams to pick up a few necessities and to get caught up in the bureaucratic whirlpool, which could be sped up or slowed down but never stopped. It had just sped up. The Hopis, I learned, were raising cain with Superintendent Edgar Miller over the definition of a "truck driver." The problem had deep roots.

President Herbert Hoover's response to the Great Depression had been to cut costs; not only had Indian Service personnel at Keams been let go, but everything was soon in short supply. The remaining bureaucrats were caught un-

prepared by Franklin D. Roosevelt and his New Deal programs, including the Indian Emergency Conservation
Work (ECW) program. Previously, agents expected they
would get only about half the items budgeted, particularly
when it came to costly items such as motor vehicles. So
quite naturally they asked for more than they needed. The
agency had, among other things, called for a small fleet of
ton-and-a-half stake-bed trucks. The new Administration
in Washington, pressured by General Motors, whose sales
were down, bought everything the agency had asked for,
resulting in a surplus of these big vehicles. So the ECW
staff members were assigned stake-bed trucks, which made
perfectly good sense for the three or four water development supervisors who hauled sacks of concrete and lengths
of pipe, but for the rest of us, who were building dams, the
trucks were simply an awkward and uncomfortable way to
get around.

When the Hopis noticed all us white men driving new
Chevrolet trucks, they called a meeting with Miller and his
staff, demanding to know why white men were being hired
to drive trucks when there were plenty of Hopis who could
drive them. Miller explained that the white foremen had
been hired not because they were truck drivers but for their
engineering and construction skills, which were essential to
their work. The Hopis simply repeated that there were
plenty of Hopi truck drivers and insisted that the white
foremen be fired and Hopi truck drivers be hired in their
place.

The impasse was solved when someone suggested there
was enough money in the agency budget to rent some cars.
The bureaucrats scurried around and persuaded some auto
dealers in Winslow and Holbrook to find enough old,
worn-out Model-A and Chevrolet coupes to rent to the

government at a handsome price. The heat was off. Now that they had cars, the white foremen could no longer be classified as truck drivers.

This incident—not atypical—almost surely served to intensify Miller's impatience with the Hopis, but it made me deeply curious. There seemed to be a wholly different logic in the Hopis' complaint. I began a running tutorial on the differences between my culture and that of both the Navajos and the Hopis. There had to be a *reality* to Hopi culture, a truth in it, for however odd their logic seemed to me, it had served them well for the near millennium they had been living on these mesas.

In general, Lorenzo was a great help in my understanding the Navajos and the Hopis, often tossing out a homespun adage with a twinkle in his eye. For example, Lorenzo said, "If a Hopi had a nickel, he would keep that nickel and squeeze it until it had babies." A Hopi wouldn't buy a wagon until he had all the money saved up, and this kind of extreme parsimony helped the Hopis to weather the depression. Not so the Navajos, who felt compelled to spend whatever money they had and to buy on credit. The Hopis' almost instinctive parsimony grew out of their long experience in this unforgiving land. It was reminiscent of the Aesop fable about the grasshopper and the ant. The ant spent the summer storing food for the winter, while the grasshopper played. When winter came, as you probably know, the grasshopper had no food.

At the time of the Spanish conquest in 1540, the Hopis occupied a core of four and then five villages: Awatovi on Antelope Mesa, well to the east of the currently occupied mesas; Walpi on First Mesa; Shongopavi on Second Mesa; and Old Oraibi at the top of Third Mesa. In 1680, in a rare show of intertribal unity, the Pueblo people along the Rio

Grande and the Hopis revolted, driving the Spanish out of what is now New Mexico and Arizona in what is known as the Pueblo Revolt. Twelve years later, in 1692, the Spanish returned with their priests and repressive government. Before the revolt there had been a large mission at Awatovi, and the Awatovi Hopis allowed the Franciscan Fathers to return to their mesa-top mission and church. The other Hopis adamantly refused to let the Spanish any farther west and felt betrayed by the Awatovis. It is possible that the other Hopis hoped that the people of Awatovi would have a change of heart and throw the priests out. But after seven winter solstices had come and gone, it was clear that nothing would change their minds. So one night a group of Hopis from several villages attacked, killing the priests and all the Awatovi men, and doled out the women and children to various villages. While the Awatovi example is perhaps the most extreme in Hopi history, throughout my stay on the Hopi reservation there were constant reminders that one of the Hopis' major problems was with each other.

Major John Wesley Powell, explorer of the Colorado River, traveled through Hopi country in the 1870s and reported that six Hopi villages and one Tewa village (Hano) occupied the tops of the mesas: Old Oraibi, Mishongnovi, Shipaulovi, Shongopavi, Walpi, and Sichomovi. The Tewas, from a Rio Grande pueblo, had been invited to settle on the Hopi mesas as a protective barrier against raiders. By the time I arrived, Polacca, Toreva, New Oraibi (Kyakotsmovi), Hotevilla, Bacabi, and Moenkopi had split off from the original six as a result of factional differences.

Hopi life was always difficult and deeply intertwined with nature. Perched high on rocky mesas and promontories in a barren, arid country, the Hopis had to carry water in jars for about a mile from springs at the base of the mesas, and they collected wood from dead junipers on the tablelands, miles away from the village. They tilled fields almost daily in the sand dunes and washes, traveling to them on foot anywhere from three to twenty miles. It was an existence on the very edge of survival, and starvation sometimes occurred. The drought and famine of the 1880s killed hundreds of Hopis, leaving an indelible mark on the memory of all I knew who were alive then. Some of the Hopis had gone crazy from hunger, hallucinating about food. One old man was seen trying to eat a piece of sandstone—thinking it was bread. The effects of this marginal, fragile, harsh existence could be seen in many aspects of Hopi life, one of which was that no Hopi felt comfortable until he had stored enough corn, dried beans, dried fruit, and squash to last through four years of drought.

A hundred miles north of the Hopi mesas lived the Ute Indians in even more marginal conditions in the desert hills. To eke out a meal, the Utes were at times forced to dig up roots and grubs and trap field mice and ground squirrels to stave off starvation. The Ute warriors' minds would turn south, centering on the Hopi women, who were soft, round, and sexy, and if that was not enough, they would think of the four-year supply of Hopi food stashed away in storage bins inside the mesa-top houses. Overwhelmed by the thought of all that food and those juicy women, the Utes would mount a raid. And if it wasn't Utes, it might be Apaches or Navajos. Clearly the Hopis had to be tough and resourceful—and they were. None of this satisfactorily explained the Hopi personality and their penchant for fighting among themselves. Of course, anyone who wants to can find an enemy nearby in a neighbor or even within the family. The Hopis seemed to have had to cope with both.

For example, not quite thirty years before my first visit to Hopi country, there was a major split at Old Oraibi. A direct result of the split was the founding of Hotevilla, a militantly conservative village, and later of Bacabi. During Superintendent Lemmon's tenure, the Hopis' equivalent of a civil war, which had been simmering below the surface, finally erupted between the old enemies—the Hostiles and the Friendlies. This surfacing of old schisms mesmerized the local whites, catching them up in its web. Government mismanagement and a lack of insight, aggravated by over-zealous missionaries, only made matters worse. Missionaries—through their continual interference in the internal affairs of the Hopis—had fanned the smoldering fires of resentment between the two factions. Having done what they could to instigate a confrontation, the missionaries then stood around wringing their hands, hoping the Friendlies would win. In the meantime, bureaucrats at Keams, thirty miles east and a day's drive in a wagon, overreacted by calling out the Army. Typically, the troops arrived over a month *after* the Hopis had settled their differences. Instead of leaving the Hopis' solution alone, the troops, aided by the superintendent's office as well as by the missionaries—all of them only too eager to punish "troublemakers"—proceeded to round up the Shongopavi Hostiles at Hotevilla, making them march back to Shongo-pavi, the village from which they had been expelled. Next, they took ninety of the Hostiles' ringleaders from the other villages and imprisoned them at Fort Wingate, east of Gallup. Most of them were heads of families. Six of the married men thought to be the most recalcitrant were sent even farther away to school in Carlisle, Pennsylvania, and weren't allowed to return to the reservation until years later. Naturally, no one thought it necessary to tell their families what had happened. Marriages dissolved when the husbands didn't return, and the wives married other men because they had no idea what had happened to their husbands.

The government harassment continued, and the missionaries, violating their own cultural mores, felt free to force entry into private homes and sacred kivas, where outsiders were not permitted. Acting as if the Hopis had no rights at all, they left no stone unturned to oppress Hopi life, sex, and religion. It is hard to believe, but even in the 1930s when I was working with them, all Indians were legally minors and were often treated as such.

I never understood, nor reconciled myself to, the government's policies concerning the treatment of Indians. I knew about the Friendly and Hostile situation, but possibly because I was only a minor player in the government game and made it a point to take the Hopis seriously, the issue did not seem to be a major factor in my work. How could it be? My job had virtually nothing to do with the political side of government-Hopi relations. I was working at the grass roots, and my business was the construction of dams and not why or where dams should be built (over which I had no control).

When Lorenzo and I talked about the Hopis, which was often, our talks revolved around what, for want of better terms, were Hopi psychology and culture, and the points that differentiated them from the Navajos and the whites. It was Hopi culture that was my primary concern, and its role was certainly more powerful than the surface manifestations of situational politics. I remember one time when a Second Mesa Hopi had come to Lorenzo wanting to sell his sheep. Asked why he wanted to sell them, the man replied, "I don't love my sheep and the sheep know it and are dying." It was typical of Lorenzo to share with me a matter with such deep implications. Some of the Hopis, as we shall see, really did not love their sheep, and the symptoms of this lack of love were easy enough to see. Some of the Hopis would leave their sheep huddled together in the corrals until long after sunup. If sheep stood too long in sheep manure mixed with the acid of urine, their hooves would soften and get sore, which made it difficult for them to travel far enough in a day to fill their stomachs. My interests may have seemed somewhat academic or even trivial to many whites, but then that was because I was genuinely interested in the people and what made them the way they were.

Still, for many whites there was a deep fascination with the Hopi mystique. Not only was there the exotic country with the Hopis' isolated villages on the mesa tops, there were the ceremonies as well. Of all the Indian dances in the Southwest, the Snake Dance is the most famous. At Snake Dance time, white people and their guests from both coasts, and even from abroad, made a pilgrimage to Hopi country. The tourists found themselves in a wild and strange environment that assaulted their senses: the sight of unbelievable distances made possible by pristine clear air, the muted gray colors of the vegetation and the intense blue of the sky. The geography was a bowl one hundred fifty miles in diameter, roughly the distance from the outskirts of Boston to the outskirts of New York City. The colors of the landscape ranged from high-key white to the pale green of the sagebrush and rabbitweed to the reddish brown of the Kayenta sandstone cliffs, punctuated here and there with sinister black basalt formations rising hundreds of feet in the air. To the south of the Hopi mesas, the intense white-hot heat of the sun could bake you to a crisp. The humidity was so low that the membranes of the nose would shrivel and crack. Most of the time, apart from the whisper of an occasional breeze passing through the rabbitweed, the chamisa, and the desert grasses, there was no sound. It never took long for the visitor to notice the near-total absence of humanity. There were occasional wagon tracks or those of a car or truck augmented by an infrequent short run of spindly poles set at different angles, carrying a single telephone line that would run parallel to the road for a short distance and then take off on its own and disappear into the desert. There were no fences unless you were observant enough to spot a field surrounded by a single strand of rusted barbed wire—hung on twisted stakes—at the foot of the Hopi mesas. There were no dwellings. On the seventy-five-mile route from Winslow to Second Mesa, the single jacal structure—made of upright posts plastered over with adobe—only accentuated the feeling of desolation. By the time the average Easterners reached Second Mesa, they were in a state now referred to as culture shock, a condition that was as hard on the Indians as it was on their visitors.

The Snake Dance occurred at different villages each year, and each dance was unique to the village. The most dramatic was Walpi's dance, suffused with mystic powers and held in a tiny plaza at the end of the mesa overlooking the three thousand square miles separating Hopi country from the railroad towns of Winslow and Holbrook.

Mishongnovi, on Second Mesa, was accessible by car with only a short walk to the dance plaza. There was space for parking and room on rooftops for everyone to get a good view of the dance. Mishongnovi's Snake Dance was not only traditional in form but endowed with enough spiritual mass to impress even the least sensitive.

The dances, in addition to the sacred part, were also a time for hospitality and entertaining. Villagers put on feasts of mutton stew, piki bread made from a blue corn-meal gruel spread thinly on a hot stone griddle, thick fry bread, and coffee with sugar and cream—all served on a large wooden table in a room jammed with friends, relatives, and an occasional Navajo or Zuni who had come to watch the dance.

The dance was preceded by eight days of secret preparation by the priests of the Snake Society, which included collecting the snakes from the surrounding desert. Then on the appointed day, with the plaza and the surrounding rooftops jammed with people who had been waiting for hours, barefoot Antelope Priests entered the plaza and formed a row. Their gleaming black hair had been let down, and they wore white cotton kilts, embroidered sashes, and necklaces of shells and beads. Each held a gourd rattle filled with seeds in his right hand. Then came the Snake Priests with their black-painted faces, white-and-red-painted bodies, and brown cotton kilts with a snake design. After circling the dance plaza several times, singing and beating out the rhythm with their feet and rattles, two groups of priests formed lines again and danced abreast. Dancing by a small bower of branches covering a hole in the ground, the pairs bent down, and each Snake Priest took a snake in his hand. The other priest then put the snake's body in the Snake Priest's mouth. This process was repeated by each pair of priests almost faster than the eye can see. The Antelope Priests, who carried feathered wands in their hands, waved them inches from the heads of the snakes to distract them. During this part of the dance, the snakes' heads would be weaving up and down and around, their long forked tongues flashing in and out. Each pair of priests might go past the bower two or three times, the priest picking out another snake, which would go in his mouth while the earlier ones were held in his hands and were free to writhe around his wrists.

The number of rattlesnakes used in this Hopi ceremony varies and depends entirely on how many were caught at the time the Snake Priests were scouring the countryside; they collected rattlesnakes, bull snakes, garter snakes, and others I was not able to identify. Occasionally a dancer would be bitten, and I once saw a dancer with blood running down his cheek. Whether it was a venomous bite I do not know. While watching the Snake Dances at various times and places, my mind was inevitably drawn to the Hopis I had known in Camp #1 who were afraid of rattlesnakes and would track down and kill any that were nearby. But then, they were not Snake Priests.

It was widely believed that the priests used various methods of milking the snakes' glands until they were free of venom. But I was never in the kiva when that happened, and I am not certain the story is true.

The climax of the dance occurred when least expected. Suddenly, the priests stopped their promenade and put their snakes on a circle of sacred cornmeal. Then the dancers scooped up the snakes and carried them in all directions to the edge of the mesa where they slithered down the mesa, taking the Hopis' prayers to Mother Earth.

The final release of the snake messengers caught most of the tourists unprepared. Elevated to a temporary high so intense, yet so brief that it was hardly experienced consciously, they would leave in a daze, hardly believing that it was over, gradually drifting toward their automobiles without really knowing what had happened. For those of us who had seen a number of these dances, we too would leave slowly, comparing notes like ballet critics.

During Snake Dance time, it was a common experience for me to be stopped by curious tourists wanting to know all about the dance. They had an unquenchable thirst for answers to such questions as "Are the snakes rattle-snakes?" "If so, how do the dancers keep from being bitten?" "If they are bitten, what keeps them from being poisoned by the venom?" "Why aren't the dancers afraid of the snakes?" "Why snakes?" I had trouble answering these questions. There seemed no way to give an answer so that there would be agreement between the statement a *Hopi might make and one the average white person would understand*. This principle applied to the totality of Hopi culture.

This was not merely a problem among tourists. When I was on the reservation, a man who had been the Oraibi School principal since the time of the Oraibi split had convinced some Hopi men to lay claim to unused Bear clan land so that they wouldn't have to walk so far—up to twenty miles a day—to till their own clan fields. The white man's logic, of which he was quite proud, was that since the fields were not being used, it was a senseless waste for them to remain fallow while the villagers of other clans were walking miles and miles to till their more-distant fields. The consequences of his white man's logic were horrendous. With all the best intentions in the world and convinced that he was doing the right, natural, logical, and just thing, the school principal in one stroke had managed to cut at the core of Hopi institutions on which everything else rested. In the simplest and most direct terms he had, without authorization or consent, donned the robe of

Tewaquaptewa, the Bear clan chief, who was also the town chief. By these acts he had interfered with the chief's sacred power to use certain special parcels of land as rewards for service to the community and for what in our terms would be considered good citizenship. Matters of this sort are not easily explained, for there are no suitable metaphors on which to anchor our thoughts.

It would be as though our President presided not only over the profane and the legal functions of governing but the sacred ones as well. And then, out of nowhere, a minor official of a foreign superpower, on the level of town clerk, suddenly injects himself into the affairs of the White House and in the process turns everything upside down, giving out favors without regard to need or merit. He confiscates land from those who own it, capriciously redistributes land without regard to land titles, birthrights, tradition, or custom, so that the indolent are rewarded at the expense of the deserving; in the process he tears the legal institution to shreds. The problem in a translation of this kind is one of culture as well as of scale. White Americans assume a relationship between size and importance, which causes us to overlook the importance of great injustices on a small scale. That was what happened at Old Oraibi.

Needless to say, the Hopis were outraged; salt had been rubbed in old wounds and the flames of old disputes had been fanned, putting the two factions—the Friendlies and the Hostiles—at each other's throats. The great inconsistency in all this was that this time it was the Hostiles who benefited from the white man's interventions while the Friendlies were being made to suffer.

When this man told me about what he had done years before, there was pride in his voice over how much trouble he had triggered by interjecting his values into a situation that obviously should have been left to the Hopis to solve for themselves.

All I could think of was the arrogance that had gone unnoticed. It had been taken for granted not only that our system was the best and the most sensible one in the world, but that we had a right to impose it on anyone in our power. I now know, however—lest I appear to be unnecessarily hard on my fellow countrymen—with the benefit bestowed by years, that it isn't just my own culture but all cultures that act in these ways. Some cultures, however, are more brutal in the process than others. Each culture has its own reasons and rationalizations for forcing its way on others. Still, even in those days I found it remarkable that after all his years of personal daily experience, Hopi thinking meant absolutely nothing to that man. He was comfortable in his own world and hadn't reached a point where it was necessary for him to change. For it would have involved grappling with such philosophical concepts as the meaning of time, which would be too great a digression to be included in this particular story. With that we leave our self-satisfied school principal smoking his pipe and perhaps wondering from time to time what all the fuss was about.

The psychologist Carl Jung held that it was sinful to interfere in the lives of others, a manifesto that is one of the most difficult of all to live by. After all that time, my school principal friend still hadn't learned that the Hopis had a right to their own system of land use and ownership, which were tied to village activities in ways he knew nothing about.

To begin with, *Hopi religion is their life.* Without it and the intertwining relationships of kachina, clan, kiva, ceremony, and land, there would be nothing. Life would be a void and without meaning. Evidences of Hopi religion were everywhere on the reservation: eagle down feathers tied in the tails of burros; painted prayer-sticks *(pahos)* with eagle down attached were placed strategically at wells, springs, fields, and shrines; men praying to the sun in the east in the early morning; the crier chief's high voice announcing the end of the day for all to hear; the sacred kivas in every village with their ladders pointing upward toward the turquoise sky, immutable and fixed like the North Star; ceremonies, dances, and sacred cornmeal. The palpable presence of religion covered and enclosed each village like an invisible dome. I could sense it when entering and leaving. It eventually came to me that the Hopi village was like a cathedral—the architecture was invisible but it was there nevertheless. White Americans and Europeans expressed their religion in their churches, temples, and cathedrals, the Hopis in *their very existence*.

Whenever you find one thing in Hopi culture, you should start looking for its complementary aspect or function. White Americans live in a dualistic, dichotomous world too, but we identify with the "good," the "right," and the "strong" and deny the "bad," the "weak," and the "dark side" in ourselves. The Hopis must incorporate both.

Dualism is a prominent feature of Hopi life/religion, which to the Hopis are inseparable. As mentioned earlier, since the advent of the whites there have been Hostile and Friendly Hopis. There are summer and winter ceremonies; Snake Dances, which alternate with Antelope Dances; masked and unmasked dances. The kachina cult—a basic component of their religion—has two divisions (Powamu and Kachina). There are two series of kachina (masked) dances: those that occur at night in the kivas during January, February, and March, and those that occur during the day in the plaza during April, May, and June. The kachinas too have their dualism. Chief kachina masks are linked to hereditary chieftaincies and are kept in the homes of the chiefs. They are never repainted and do not generally appear in the public dance plaza as part of the dance group. All the rest of the kachinas can be roughly classed in groups, usually with their own kind, and all are repainted each year.

Then there were the witches, who were called *two hearts*. Witchcraft is present in most if not all cultures and is never easy to explain. But one of the great paradoxes of Hopi life was a "belief" they held concerning old age. Aging was not easy or natural to the Hopis but was seen as coming at the expense of the life force drawn from others. This must have been a dreadful burden for them to carry. In case you are thinking, "But that doesn't make sense. How can it be? How could an old person get vitality by stealing it from someone who is young?" Answer: It is possible if he or she is a witch—a two hearts.

At the same time, the Hopi prayers at baby-naming ceremonies call for a long life, and the ideal is to grow old and bent until one's forehead touches the ground so that one can go into the next life. I am left with the assumption that this is another case of Hopi duality—a trait that is present to some degree in most if not all cultures.

Patterns of belief and behavior of this sort, like Jung's light and dark sides, are not always easy to explain. For one thing the people themselves never know all there is to know about themselves, nor can they give satisfactory descriptions of the unwritten, unstated, tacit rules governing their lives. This doesn't mean they don't talk about these things; they do. Culture, however, is the last frontier, and the world beyond that frontier is unbelievably intricate and complex. There are a grammar and a vocabulary for every human act—dreams, for example, and myths, both of which are frequently dismissed as trivial meanderings of the mind. Even so-called psychotics are far from insane, once it is known what is going on in their perceptual systems.

We say and believe one thing on one level underneath which is another pattern that more often than not is denied. It takes courage to see ourselves as we really are. This was best illustrated by a man I used to know—albeit casually—Don Talayesva, Sun Chief of Old Oraibi, who found himself as an old man fearing that his dreams about two hearts might actually be true. Personally, I have had too much experience with cultures in which witchcraft is present ever to dismiss it as an aberration of the mind and therefore removed from reality. The task of the human species is to try as best we can to understand each other and not dismiss something simply because we don't believe it, or because the subject of our disbelief is not present in our own culture and is treated as a superstition.

To return to dualities: the Hopi religious calendar is divided in half by the summer and winter solstices. The Kachina ceremonies begin following the winter solstice and last until July. After the summer solstice a particularly moving, poignant dance, the Niman kachina, or Home Dance, is given. It is at this time that the kachinas leave the Hopi mesas for their home in the San Francisco Peaks, visible on the horizon from the mesas, one hundred miles southwest (just north of Flagstaff). The Hopi masked dancers performed their sacred rite, saying good-bye to the village on one side, while behind them in the blue outline are the distant San Francisco Mountains. The dancers were not just Indians dressed up like kachinas, but they embodied the spirits of the kachinas. Whenever I saw the dance, I couldn't help thinking what it must be like to have the gods with you, an integral part of your daily life one moment, and then suddenly to have them leave! This is the kind of cultural difference that was beyond my ability to comprehend. A thousand years of anthropology could not explain it to me because there was nothing in my experience to hook it to. As an American of European heritage, I had been brought up to know that people had something called beliefs. Beliefs were like a suit of clothes. You could change your beliefs. But having the gods with you in a dance and in your daily life was something else—much deeper than mere belief—which may have explained some of our trouble understanding the Indians. We could not accept that many aspects of their lives went beyond belief and instead were organic, an integral part of their nature.

Of all the Hopi artifacts, the most interesting and ultimately the most mysterious are the kachina dolls. These small figures, carved from the soft roots of the cottonwood tree, were painted in bright earth colors and given to children by the masked dancers along with an admonition or lesson about Hopi life. They are the material manifestations of Hopi values and are traditionally hung on the walls of the home as reminders of what is right and decent as well as what to avoid. I often wondered: what are these values? Nothing I heard about the kachina dolls quite made sense. My intuition told me that in these crudely carved figures of the masked kachina dancers there would be some deep clues to the rest of Hopi culture. The more I dug into the subject, the more obvious it became that my own categories simply did not fit the Hopis.

There are between two hundred fifty and four hundred

varieties of kachinas, depending on the source consulted. To the children, the kachina dancers are real in somewhat the same way Santa Claus is to white children. They are real to adults too, but in a different way in that the masked dancers, while known as dancers, are also seen as the embodiment of the kachina spirits. In matters of this kind we must proceed further and look at the deeper levels of culture, the levels beneath what we think of as "beliefs." White culture demands that we categorize, as well as define, events and material manifestations of our belief systems technically; Hopi culture does not. In our religious and occult categories, we find supernatural beings—deities, gods, devils, ghosts, spirits, elves, fairies, gnomes. We inevitably try to force the kachinas into one or more of these categories. Not all kachinas are gods nor are they just nature spirits, as I once thought. They are archetypes representing virtually everything impinging on Hopi life. They are material metaphors for the Hopi ethos and seem to be related to the tacit side of culture—the very subject I was beginning to study, the very reason I had been attracted to them in the first place.

The point is that these are not just dolls or even totemic images of animal spirits. As a whole, they are an important statement of life, and life to the Hopis means religion. Life changes, so the inventory of kachinas changes. Some are dropped, new ones are added. Eventually the kachina doll became a metaphor for what I did not know about the Hopis. So now I hang them on my wall just as the Hopi children do, to remind me that in the eyes of God I am a child, to remind me of my relationship with the Hopis and of all that I do not know—not only about the Hopis but about everything else.

6

The Fragility
of Understanding

ONCE POSTED TO ORAIBI, I made a habit of dropping by to see Lorenzo, and on an early occasion he took my arm and led me through the office door to his bedroom and then into the kitchen, where we would not be disturbed. In his gravelly voice, he told me that since I didn't speak Navajo, I would need an interpreter on my new job and that the government had money for that sort of thing. Here was another instance of Lorenzo's taking care of things, even seeing to it that the government's work progressed in the best possible manner—mainly for the Indians but also for the government.

In my new role as construction foreman—dam builder—

I had reported to a man named Shultz, a recent arrival on the ECW staff, compliments of the United States Irrigation Service, and as bilious a man as I have ever met. His first words had been a string of profanity followed by imperious shouts and threats to the effect that if I made any trouble, he would "kick my ass." He then curtly told me I would be in charge of three dam projects—one near Blue Canyon with a Navajo crew and two others, elsewhere, with Hopi crews. I learned later that sight unseen, he was infuriated because he had hoped to put one of his relatives in my position. Naturally, neither he nor any other bureaucrat in the Keams hierarchy was about to suggest that money was available for an interpreter.

Lorenzo made it plain that not just any old interpreter would do. The interpreter would represent me, he would *be* me in a way. It was essential that there be a rapport between us. After all, we would be bouncing around, shut up together in the hot dusty cab of a truck all day. He would represent me as the one who was in charge, and he had to be able to translate my thinking accurately and honestly. Ideally, and on some occasions, the interpreter and I would be almost one person.

There were many things in Navajo that didn't translate into English and vice versa; for this reason, the interpreter should be able to rephrase what I had said in English so that it came out the way it should in Navajo. I knew what seemed simple to me might not be so simple when translated into Navajo. Lorenzo didn't explain this to me and it would not have been like him to do so. However, I had lived not only in France, where I did have at least some command of the language, but also in New Mexico, where I had extensive experience with the Tewa pueblos of Tesuque, San Ildefonso, and Santa Clara. I was accustomed to seeing and hearing a long harangue only to have the interpreter say, "He said no." I was aware that the interpreter might not be able to translate a given thought into English or that to translate that thought would have taken too long. These things I knew, accepted, and took on faith. Also, Lorenzo was not a linguist. He just knew the language and the culture; in fact, he was fluent in both. But he could not have explained the difference, which was the task for well-trained linguistic scientists who had worked with the language for years. Lorenzo did mention from time to time that the Navajo language was very precise and capable of fine shades of meaning that went way beyond both Spanish and English.

Lorenzo said he had given a good deal of thought to who would be best as my interpreter on the reservation. Having started with a list of eight or nine men, he had narrowed the list to two men and then ruled out one of the two best-qualified candidates because he was apt to be "political," which I took to mean opportunistic and self-serving. This left a young Navajo, Sam Yazzie, from the west side of the Dinnebito Wash where some of my jobs were located. Lorenzo told me that Sam was from one of the strongest well-known families on the reservation, which meant that his people had lots of horses and sheep and were doing well above average economically speaking, as well as being respected and even feared. He also thought it good that the two of us were about the same age.

By then I was beginning to be a little cautious concerning my expectations. Normally I would have been bursting with impatient excitement to meet Sam. But since a good deal of my expectations in the past had proved to be wide of the mark, I adopted a wait-and-see attitude.

The next Monday, a thin, pleasant-looking young man

of medium height entered the outside door to Lorenzo's office. His entry was followed by a long conversation with Lorenzo in Navajo with Sam giving the appropriate *O'h, O'h's,* meaning yes, yes. I could tell they were talking about me because of references to *Chiz Chili,* my Navajo name. While all this was going on, I followed my usual custom of sitting there passively, watching and picking up what I could by the way they were talking. Following what seemed to be an endless set of instructions, Lorenzo turned to me and said with very little ceremony, "This is Sam Yazzie, the man I told you about. He is very reliable." At which point we shook hands in the white man's way, which meant we looked each other in the eye. I asked Sam if he was ready to go to work and told him that my truck was outside.

He said, "Let's go." His selection of that particular expression without any noticeable accent, and the speed and ease of his reply, told me that my chances for his having a high degree of fluency in English were excellent and that I had little to fear from that direction. The rest—all the points made by Lorenzo—I would know only after we had worked together.

My expectations this time were less than what fate served me on a silver platter. A great many Indians in those days were shy and ill at ease with whites—and no wonder. As it turned out, it would have been impossible to find a more apt and compatible tutor and guide to the ins and outs of Navajo culture and psychology than Sam. He was young, articulate, cheerful, energetic, highly intelligent, curious, and, while easygoing, willing to work. He was well connected in his community, meaning that he had lots and lots of relatives of good reputation and affluence. Also, he had a knack for doing things right. Yet with all of this, I could see that he was still all Navajo, from his skin to the center of his soul and from the top of his head to the soles of his feet.

We hit it off immediately; in fact, we took great pleasure in each other's company. The lack of anxiety had a good deal to do with it. Neither of us made the other anxious or angry. We didn't push each other but let matters unfold naturally. But I think it may have been a matching of body rhythms that was as much a factor as anything else. Respect is another factor of paramount importance. If you don't respect others, how can you possibly get along? We were both intensely interested in what we each knew about our own way of doing things. What we lacked was a shared background of common experience. In this sense, we really were strangers to each other. And with strangers my tendency has always been to avoid pushing and to try to remain alert until I have categorized the other person in some way. My impression was that Sam, too, had to feel me out until I fit into one of his as-yet-to-be-discovered categories.

My tutorial with Sam Yazzie began the first time the two of us climbed into our truck. After I slammed my ill-fitting door, he turned around, looked at his door, and pulled it quietly shut. After I had slammed my door a couple of more times and he had pulled his shut quietly, I began to get the point.

Sam was deeply curious about the world I came from, which may seem strange to today's reader because with radio, TV, and the press, information is ubiquitous. In the thirties, however, even I had to keep reminding myself that here was a nation of people living in another century who not only did not speak English but many of whom had met maybe five or fewer white people. Some of Sam's questions puzzled me, and given that he was so fluent in English, I wondered about the schools that would teach him so little of the customs of the people who surrounded him on all sides. His questions, however, came from his experience and not mine. For example, one time we were driving along, bouncing across the desert landscape, and out of the blue he asked me, "How much did you pay for your wife?" The Navajos have an institution called the bride price. It wasn't that they bought their women but that the bride's family must be reimbursed for the loss of a useful, productive member of their group. I gathered that a young man of my age was expected to be married, and I had to explain— somewhat apologetically, I might add—that I didn't have a wife and that we white men got our wives for nothing, which in the context of the conversation made me feel sort of cheap. He found this hard to believe, because a wife was a valuable asset and brought with her properties like sheep and sometimes even horses. He also wanted to know how our government was organized, and I did my best to explain this without making invidious comments about the people at Keams.

The questions seemed a little odd, since I was not used to that kind of interest in our government from an Indian. This young man, who was fast becoming my friend, wanted to know how our country was put together and run. He was using me as an informant. Not too many whites, even those who have spent a good deal of time visiting over the years with the Hopis and the Navajos, have found themselves in my situation. Sam could see that the world was beginning to change. One of the signs of this change was my presence on the reservation. Nevertheless, something about his questions suggested an agenda. I could see the outlines of an idea beginning to form. And then, quite without warning, this idea took shape.

One day Sam and I were riding cross-country on horse-back to look at a dam site that was easier to reach by horse than by car. Just as we crested the top of a low ridge, silhouetted against the sky were four Navajo men on horseback waiting for us. Putting spurs to their horses, they rode up and joined us. By their dress, their jewelry, and their horses, I noted immediately that these were not ordinary men. They were bedecked in turquoise and silver jewelry, fine new shirts, and Levis. Their saddles were well kept, not repaired with bailing wires as were most of the saddles I had seen. Instead of the more common small, almost pony-size horses, their horses were big for our country, perhaps as much as one thousand pounds. But it was the jewelry, belts, bracelets, bow guards, which were the tip-off to the affluence and power of these men.

I should explain that I had owned horses, lived on ranches, and knew about tack as well as about horses. It was still a time when the kind of horse a man rode was as much a mark of status as today's automobiles, boats, and airplanes. To dig a little deeper: properly read, the way a horse and tack were cared for was generally a reliable indicator of character and answered such questions as did the man care? Was he careful? Did he think about the future by saving his horse and maintaining his tack? Loose or worn-out cinches could cost a life if they broke while you were roping a steer. Your fate and that of your horse were intimately and functionally related.

But it was chiefly the posture and the bearing of these four men that suggested to me they were local headmen and that this was no casual meeting. These were big shots. I learned later from Sam that they were *natanis*—headmen, and thinkers as well. In an uncharacteristic manner for Navajos, they wasted no time getting down to business.

As we rode cross the landscape, they questioned me not about the ECW projects and my work but about my society and culture. Their questions were well formulated and penetrating, and I could see that they had devoted deep thought to the subjects to be covered during my interrogation. They wanted to know how whites settled disputes, how we defined health, happiness, and beauty (which I knew by then to be a central theme in Navajo cultural doctrines). How was our government organized? How did we choose our representatives and judges? They would be specific and detailed at times. They wanted to know if men (women were not so common in government as they are today, so they were only asking about men) in our government were paid and how old did you have to be before you could be President? We got into demographics. How many of us were there? There were around 125 million persons in the United States at that time, but I had trouble explaining what this number meant, even to the Navajos, who at 50,000 (today they number 250,000) were the most numerous of all our Indian tribes. I explained all this as best I could by translating some of what I told them into what I knew of their own thought frames, which was not as much as I would have liked. During the entire process I kept saying to myself, "If I only knew more, not only about them but of my own culture."

The contemporary reader may wonder why these men did not learn the answers to their questions in school. The answer lies in history. I was being queried in 1933. If these men, whose average age was in the fifties, had been able to attend school, it would have been in the late nineteenth century at a time when there were no schools for the

Navajos. I did know, for example, that Clare G., a Navajo from Pinyon, and Byron Adams, a First Mesa Hopi missionary, were the first boys from the reservation to attend school because they ran away *to* school together. I never did find out the exact date, but Clare and Byron were in their late thirties or early forties when I knew them. Enforced education for the reservation Indian children probably didn't begin until after World War I. "Schoolboys," who wore their hair short, were in their early twenties and were still not a common sight on the reservation.

Two and a half hours after our horseback seminar had started, the four *natanis* turned their horses off to the side, said good-bye, and rode away, leaving me mentally and physically exhausted—but also somehow inspired. The fact that the entire interrogation occurred on horseback as we rode across sagebrush, mesquite, and gama grass under the massive western sky gave the transaction a dynamic power. During those two and a half hours there would be moments when, cresting a ridge, I could see as far north as Navajo Mountain on the Arizona-Utah border, over ninety miles away. But what I couldn't see, because they didn't tell me, was what lay behind all those questions.

What I did learn was something of how the Navajo mind works, which was later supported not only by Lorenzo but by specialists in the field like Clyde Kluckhohn. Other qualities, however, were only hinted at, and I couldn't help but wonder about the minds that could come up with such a repertoire of questions. The *natanis* had struck me as smarter than many of my college professors. They acted as though the information they were after was vitally important. Were they trying to put together a government? Was this information useful to them in developing strategies for coping with white culture? I never knew, but I continued to dwell on the high quality of mind I had encountered. It occurred to me then, and many times since, that white society certainly had failed to use what was there before us, just waiting—in fact begging—to be applied. When all is said and done, we still don't know how to use such talents creatively. Identifying the talents of the unusual, even in our own society, has never been the strong point of American culture. Everything inevitably ends up in the hands of a bureaucracy instead of in the hands of gifted individuals.

When I had something to say to one of my Navajo foremen, Sam and I would go over it first to be sure I had the correct message and that Sam understood it well enough to make it clear in Navajo. When a Navajo was talking to me and there were long passages of words followed by a short interpretation from Sam, such as "He said yes," I would wait until we were on the road again away from the crew to question him at length about what had really been said. Sam would usually tell me, providing insights into a new, strange, and entirely different world. It is not possible for me to give an adequate treatise on the influence of language on thought and the relation between language and culture—complex subjects first explored by the linguist Edward Sapir—but I could intuit the process unfolding before my eyes (and ears).

Leslie Marmon Silko's book *Ceremony* provides us with an excellent, as well as subtle, example of how a Pueblo Indian approaches language and the effect it has on the way in which language is used.

The situation described by Silko involves two Laguna Indian people: an older medicine man and a young Indian warrior who has returned from the Vietnam war in a state of shock and disintegration. Silko describes how the older man, looking into the eyes of the young warrior, begins by telling him how *fragile* and intricate the *world* is. Then the old man explains the *meaning* of the word fragile and how *no word exists alone*. That there is a *story* behind each word and how essential it is to use each word so that there is "no mistake in the meaning of what has been said . . ."

The example is simple as well as brief, but if the reader will carefully compare in his or her own mind how language is used by a Laguna Pueblo Indian with a comparable situation in which an older white male is comforting and counseling a young war veteran, this example should take on additional meaning. The most significant difference is that most people in our schools tend to be quite casual about language, and we certainly don't think that it is necessary to open a discussion with a younger person with an analysis of language.

Yet much that took place between Sam and me was influenced by this very same language factor. My situation was different from that of the shell-shocked warrior. I was learning from scratch so that much that took place between Sam and me as a team and my Navajo crews was acquired pretty much in the same way the child acquires language—without conscious knowledge. For the first time in my life, I was left with a sense of the inherent order in culture in how people go about understanding and acting in their world—and not in just one culture but all cultures. I was gradually being transformed from an immature adult into a man. Navajo culture became a part of my very being. Already, I found myself avoiding eye contact when close to others or talking to them. Already, I was synchronizing my body movements with the Navajo rhythm and tempo, which I found to be smoother and more coordinated than my own (most whites move rather jerkily). Already, I was learning how to enter and leave situations and how to comport myself in ways congruent with those of the Navajos. As in learning a new language, I did not see these adaptations as giving up any part of my own personality, which is a common fear of many Americans and their excuse for not taking other cultures seriously. I learned this in real life situations years later when training technicians for work in the third world, but the foundation was laid back there in the early thirties while working with the Navajos. I discovered that as I began to acquire more and more of the overt patterns of Navajo behavior, life became smoother and more rewarding, which is difficult to explain. How do you describe the subtle differences in an office when things are going well and when they are not? It was this sort of change I noted. Also, I was simply more at ease with my crews, more relaxed, more a part of the total situation. There was less difference between us than before.

In summary, I had been given some new forms for dealing with strangers that would last me the rest of my life. Adjusting your tempo to that of a new country does make a difference. If you adjust your distances to theirs, as well as your eye behavior, you are communicating a kind of kindred spirit that makes your alien presence easier to take. These are actions the peoples of the world need to know right now. They are covered in the books I wrote years after my baptism in the fire of intercultural relations among my Indian brothers and sisters. There are other things I learned too, which I can talk about now that the foundation has been laid.

There was no way to sneak up on a job on our regular rounds. Our vehicles made enough noise grinding along across the mesas that our crews could hear us coming for at least thirty or forty minutes before we arrived. It certainly was not necessary to announce our presence. However, having arrived, we stopped and turned off the motor. I would let Sam take the initiative in timing our descent from the truck. Watching him, I learned that even in such matters as making our presence known, there were preferred ways of entering into any and all transactions. Though we whites thought nothing of it, we were abrupt and usually made sure that considerable noise and fuss accompanied entrances. Wherever we whites were, we knocked on doors, rang bells, honked horns, or just plain let out a holler when we came within hailing distance.

To the Navajo, the proper entry was different and a matter to which they paid particular attention. Their ideal way of making an entrance was to ease in, to make their approach as well as their presence subtle and harmonious. Navajos would sing a barely audible song when approaching a hogan so that the people inside would know they were about to be visited and have time to prepare themselves mentally. If the person inside was sleeping, the song would allow time for the soul to return to the body.

Sam and I would let our presence sink in gradually so that the crew could make the necessary mental and emotional adjustments. The signal for us to descend from the truck was when the foreman walked over slowly in the ambling gait so characteristic of Navajo men when they are not in a hurry. The foreman's name was Stutter; his name translated to the Tall Man Who Stutters. His shiny black hair was pulled back and tied in a neat bun at the back of his head, traditional Navajo style. Well over six feet tall, Stutter had an easy disposition and exuded a quiet competence. A leader among his own people, he was also recognized as such among whites. As he approached, Sam timed our slow descent from the truck so as to be standing comfortably in place on the ground at the moment of his arrival.

Stutter then escorted us to the job, the work stopped, and everyone would take a break. Smoking played a ceremonial role among the Indians then. The crew made a big circle, and since I did not have a ceremonial pipe, I produced the makings—tobacco in a can and Wheat Straw paper to roll cigarettes. The order was always the same. Arrive, wait for things to settle down, greet the foreman, let the crew rest and form a circle, pass the makings around, smoke, enjoy, fill in the time book, discuss the work and anything that had happened since the last visit, go over and inspect the job, greet each man as he passed with his team, and then, when everything had been attended to, take our departure.

This ceremonious routine helped me become a part of the Navajo world and begin to work the Indians' world into my own. Taking my cues from Lorenzo and Sam, I thought it only sensible to do things the Navajo way, even if it meant some discomfort on my part. This did not mean going native, but it did mean showing respect by avoiding eye contact, for example, when talking to a Navajo, speaking with a soft voice, entering a store in such a way as not to disturb the air, waiting in the truck for the people to come out of a hogan—for they might not be ready to see someone. The Navajo's greeting and the white man's greeting were not the same. White males (and now most white females) grip the proffered hand firmly—at times too firmly for my taste—looking the other party directly in the eye, all of which is intended to convey interest, honesty, and sincerity. But when we would do this to the Navajos, it conveyed quite a different message; a direct, unwavering gaze meant anger. Of course, Navajos who have frequent contact with outsiders have become accustomed to our way of doing things by now, so for some, this is no longer an issue. But it is not difficult to see why Navajos had the impression that most whites were perpetually angry and ill-natured. The Navajo greeting does not center on showing relative strength and dominance (as it does with two Anglo males) but is instead a communication in which there is a mutual assessment of feelings and expression. As two men approach each other, eye contact is broken—at about the point where it is possible to begin to pick up the details of facial expression. Once this boundary is crossed, they look past each other, holding the approaching figure in their peripheral field of vision. To look directly at the other is tantamount to swearing at them (to a child, a sharp look takes the place of a hard slap). The handshake is gentle and is held for quite a while—held but not squeezed—as each soaks up the emotional tone of the other. When each has both sent and received the warmth and pleasure of meeting as well as a sampling of each others' underlying mood, then they have in a subtle way also communicated mutual respect. It didn't take me long to get into this greeting style and the warm feelings that went with it.

When I returned to my own society two years later, it was almost a year before I could break myself of the habit of looking beyond the person to whom I was speaking. My adjustment to Navajo ways went beyond the behavioral and into the psychological side of their culture. I had to learn to avoid reliance on logic and switch to a quid pro quo type of relating. I had to accentuate the present, the practical, and the instrumental, avoiding references to future rewards. In particular, I learned to accentuate the value of harmony as well as to avoid changes in my way of doing things. In the process, I soon acquired the habit of sensing people's feelings and returning those feelings with my own, and I learned to avoid negative feelings. In a word, I had to learn to tune into their world and keep in mind that my world and my natural way of doing things were frequently antithetical to theirs.

I should explain that in the white person's culture, particularly today, most of our information is gleaned from what other people tell us in words, supplemented by pictures from the TV tube, and that our way of getting information is by asking questions, an art with its roots in Socrates and Plato. In fact, dependence on the word *paradigm* has been part of the European tradition since that time. The Indians in the Southwestern part of the United States have one belief in common, which I fortunately picked up at an early age from my Tewa friends: questions not only are *not* a good way to get information but are actually intrusive, as though we were taking over the mind of the other, which is what a question does. Questions put the other person's mind in a vice and act like a curb bit in a horse's mouth. Because I was not brought up speaking Navajo and have never been good at picking up languages quickly, I learned only enough to get around, be polite, go with the flow, and okay the work to be done. By avoiding questions, I simply did what the Indians do; I emphasized the use of my eyes and ears and the gray matter in between. Since somewhere between 85 and 90 percent of communication between humans and virtually all communication between animals is of the nonverbal, highly contextualized variety, I had a rich field to study that avoided the distortions of words and the discomfort of intruding. Needless to say, cultural material gathered in this way is different from what we get from questions. This does not mean that words should be eliminated from the investigative tool kit. In fact, quite the contrary. When a man tells us the story of his life or describes something that happened, we learn to pay attention. It is quite clear to me, however, that my work with the Navajos had a deep influence on, in fact established the foundation for, my later work in *nonverbal communication*.

In all of this, it took me a while to become aware of my own cultural baggage. In the eyes of the white man, there was no need for ceremony when driving up to a construction site—in fact, just the opposite. Another set of manners was in vogue. To whites, the reservation job sites were in a "man's world," far away from the "wipe your feet, don't slam the door" world of women. The Anglo image of the construction foreman, as epitomized by Shultz, called for a display of the freedom from mom, schoolteachers, and wives. Men whose primary objective, without realizing it, was to show their subordinates who was in charge, and their importance, made a lot of noise. (Among chimps, making noise establishes a number one status.) The Anglo foreman would drive up in a hurry, leaving a cloud of dust in his wake. When he came to a stop, he honked the horn to let the crew know he had arrived. Having listened to the talk among some of our foremen and their supervisors, I could see that behind the exaggerated pose of the big shot was a kind of ethnic put-down, an attitude that said, "I'm going to show these Indians what it means to be a real man." Of course, what constitutes appropriate male and female behavior is determined by the culture of one's upbringing, but almost none of the white supervisors in the ECW had the remotest clue about that. Instead, they assumed that their way of doing things was the only normal way for a human being to act. Seen through Navajo eyes, our white foremen, with all their shouting and noise, instead of demonstrating masterly strength, communicated just the opposite.

Apart from helping to dredge a pond on my father's place in Missouri, I had little experience with earth moving, so I placed my trust in my foremen, my crews, and Sam. The basic plan for all the dams was a 3:1 slope on the upriver side, a 2:1 slope on the downriver side, with a ten-foot-wide flat crown and walkway across the top. The work progressed slowly. At times it appeared that little progress had been made at all since the last visit. Of course the base of a dam, which is laid down first, is the largest, most spread-out part—the part with the most dirt. As the dam progresses, less and less dirt is required for each foot in height. Actually, a dam doesn't even begin to look like a dam until it is almost finished. I had in my mind a picture of a finished dam, and there was always tension between what I saw and what I hoped would be the end results. I used to wonder how my crews managed to place the dirt so that the slopes maintained an even gradient. I fretted about what would happen if a flash flood wiped out one of my jobs before it was finished. One day on a visit to Keams, one of the Shockleys (the engineers who had surveyed and laid out the dams) told me, "That's all part of the game. It's bound to happen. We won't hold it against you. After all, you can't control the weather, and we expect that when the rains come, we'll lose a few dams."

Life on the reservation had a way of following a routine and then, when you had adjusted and least expected it, it exploded in your face. I soon learned to try to think ahead and foresee the possible consequences of even the most trivial events. For instance, the day their first paychecks were issued, my crews rejoiced. For the first time in several years, there was a little extra money left after paying something down on the trader's account. The near-starvation level of poverty of the preceding years had not allowed enough money to pay the medicine man and provide food for the sings, or curing ceremonies, that were one of the central features of Navajo life. Now they could afford a sing.

The important sings lasted up to nine days and reaffirmed life, health, and community relationships. Even those who couldn't get there for the actual event wanted to participate in some way. Once, while driving across the Dinnebito Flats, I could just barely see a Navajo running toward me from over a mile away. Out in the open country, whenever I saw a man running, I knew he could want only one thing—for me to stop and wait. Usually it was to ask for a job, sometimes it was to take a message to the trader. One time it was to find out when school was out, so they could be at Oraibi when their children were brought back after a long absence at a boarding school some thousand miles away. This time, panting, a Navajo stuck his head in the window of my car and asked, "Where will the prayer plume be traveling tonight? I want to follow it with my thoughts." At first I was stumped. Then I remembered hearing that a Mountain Chant up near Black Mountain store was in progress. Digging still further, I remembered vaguely that I had overheard someone say something about Blue Gap. The effectiveness of a sing was dependent, in addition to the power and skill of the medicine man, on community participation. Everybody put thoughts into the collective pot to help with the cure, even if it meant running for miles on the chance that a white man on the road between Oraibi and Tuba City might have heard where a prayer plume was going for a sing, which was several hours' drive to the northeast.

Stutter's dam was within three miles of where the sing was being performed. The last day of the sing—the most important day to attend—the crew asked for the day off. Knowing they would take it anyway, Sam and I decided that it would be better to grant permission than to say no and then pretend that everyone was on the job when we knew they were not.

Late the next afternoon I returned to my house in Oraibi from my Hopi job to the south. I found a message tacked to the door telling me to get over to Lorenzo's office without delay. Three minutes later I opened the door to Lorenzo's darkened office, where I was greeted by an earth-shaking blast of violent profanity that rocked me back on my feet. By the time my eyes adjusted to the dark, I could see my boss, Shultz, sitting across from Lorenzo, his face contracted in a hideous mask of rage. Listening to his tantrum, I managed to piece together the cause. Stutter's dam had been hit by a flash flood while the Indians were away dancing!

"It's going to be your ass, Hall, believe me. This will cost your job. There's no way I can save you, and I'm not even going to try. You get your butt out there right now and get that dam fixed. I mean right now. Don't wait until morning."

"Yes, sir. Anything else?"

"No! Now get the hell out of here!"

There was still enough daylight left at the site to assess the damage, which was restricted to the central portion of the dam. A narrow trench had been cut through the soft, freshly laid earth, but it could be fixed. Had the flood hit a week later, there would have been no problem, for by then there would have been enough earth on top to have channeled any surplus runoff to one side over the spillway. I calculated that the single day lost while the crew was away couldn't have made the slightest difference; the dam would have washed out anyway. Since all the dams were built in drainages for the specific purpose of catching the very kind of runoff that had washed this one out, there had always been a calculated risk. In my two years of building dams, this was the only one I ever lost.

Since there was nothing further to be done right then, Sam and I attended the last night of the Yeibichai (Mountain Chant) ceremony, one of the most impressive of all Navajo ceremonies. It was a masked ceremony that had lasted seven days and nights. During the day sand paintings were made in the hogan by the medicine men. The patient sat in the middle of the hogan while the sand painting drew off the illness and at the same time permitted the power of the painting to flow into the patient's body. At dusk the painting was destroyed. The singing and dancing outside the hogan went from dusk to dawn.

Repairing the damage to the dam was relatively simple. Rather than piling in new dirt that would rest on the washed-out channel, Stutter cut a wedge-shaped slot into the bottom and each side of the original channel so that the new fill would be keyed into solid earth. Later, looking at the finished dam, I could see that the crown was straight and true, exactly ten feet wide at all places (the Navajos had cut a sapling ten feet long as a guide). The slopes were even. The front face was 2:1, just the way it should be, and the rear face, as smooth as a table and stopping where the stakes had been, was a more gradual 3:1. This was my first dam, but it was Stutter's first as well. I also knew that a comparably inexperienced crew of whites could not have achieved such a high level of perfection, nor would they have been expected to. From the beginning the Navajos clearly had carried a three-dimensional picture in their heads of how the dam should look when finished. Working along day by day, they followed hidden lines that told them at what point to stop adding dirt.

The finishing process was extraordinary. Using the simplest of improvised scraping, smoothing, and leveling tools, they made all three surfaces smooth and level— front, top, and back—not just smooth but tabletop smooth. Then, to cut down on erosion, they riprapped the entire rear face of the dam, as well as the spillway, with thin, neatly fitted sheets of shale. The meticulous Navajos again did a magnificent job. Not only were all the stones even, but they all fit together perfectly, as in a well-laid flagstone walk. It was clear from the beginning that quality and attention to detail were very important to my Indian crews, and that there was nothing academic about it.

As I watched this process unfold, I was reminded that my archaeologist friends and colleagues at Mesa Verde and Chaco Canyon had told me how the Navajos could reproduce exactly any type of masonry found in the ruins and were the best masons available for reconstruction work in such sites.

My experience with the Navajos on that first dam was repeated time and time again all over the reservation. It made me wonder why the government didn't make better use of the Navajos' talents. It was clear that they were being wasted.

Nothing more was said about the washout of the dam. Shultz was later transferred back to the Irrigation Service, where he belonged, taking with him my very fine Ithaca double-barreled shotgun he had borrowed from me. I heard nothing more from him. Lorenzo, feeling that I needed cheering up, kidded me about Shultz's rage at the time of the washout.

"By God, I've never seen anything like it. Did you ever see the face of a skinned bobcat? His face looked just like the face of a skinned bobcat!"

My first dam was as close to perfect as it was possible to get, not because I knew so much but because I knew so little and, knowing that, didn't oversupervise. Stutter's success may have had to do with the harmony in which we all worked, for harmony is a vitally important element in Navajo life. When there is harmony, things go right; in its absence, things go wrong.

7

The Navajos

IT WAS 1929, and I was taking my meals at Mrs. Jensen's boardinghouse on Canyon Road while attending high school in Santa Fe, New Mexico. We were barely into the school year when our table was joined by two Park Service employees from Mesa Verde, site of the famous Anasazi cliff ruins in Colorado. One, a short, well-muscled young man named Kenny Wallace, was a construction foreman recuperating from a horrendous accident that befell him in the forest a few miles from the park headquarters. He and a Navajo crew had been using a tractor to clear a right-of-way for a forest road by pulling the stumps of felled trees. The procedure was to hook a chain around a stump, put the tractor in reverse, and slowly back up, being careful not to snap the chain by putting too much pressure on it at any given moment. It was shortly after the noon break when one of the roots unexpectedly came loose. The tractor lurched and Kenny fell off the back while the tractor was still in motion. Landing behind the tractor, he was rolled—over and over underneath the tractor—with only a few inches of clearance, all the while miraculously maintaining consciousness. He could hear his bones being broken and didn't give himself a "snowball's chance in Hell" of surviving. But just as his head emerged from the front of the tractor, which was still in reverse and attached to the stump, he saw his Navajo crew start to run as though the Devil himself was after them. The flight told Kenny that his crew thought he was dead and therefore *chindi*—contaminated and dangerous. Seeing the rapidly approaching stump being pulled by the driverless tractor, Kenny called to his crew in Navajo—none of them spoke English then—telling them how to shut the motor off. (He told me that he had to hand it to his crew, because when they discovered he was alive, they scampered back and were able to stop the tractor.) With that emergency taken care of, another just as serious loomed. He had been trucking his crew in a Dodge Power Wagon, which looked like a green grocer's truck, to the work site over a virtually impassable mountain road. Knowing he couldn't drive and probably shouldn't even be moved, he thought the only solution—albeit "risky as all get out"—was to direct the men in the delicate task of easing him into the front seat of the truck, beside the driver's seat, without puncturing a lung or severing an artery in one of his broken limbs. This move was finally accomplished while one of his crew held him upright in his seat from behind.

It was then that the real tour de force began. We have all heard the stories of nonpilots who land planes when the pilot is disabled, "talked down" by the steady, properly sequenced instructions of another pilot's voice on the radio. The voice on the radio in the plane is speaking the language both are born to, referring to knobs and buttons and gauges, which are something like what they have seen in their cars. But think for a moment what this would be like if you were crippled in the plane and had to do it in Navajo with someone at your side who has never driven any piece of power machinery before. In the forest near Mesa Verde, Kenny Wallace was in such a position, and he was in a backcountry location, which required consummate driving skill even when the driver was in full control of not only his senses but his limbs as well. Thinking all this over and realizing there was only one thing to do, Kenny picked a man who he had noted was particularly attentive to what Kenny had been doing while driving. He asked the man if he thought he could drive the *chidi* (automobile) down the mountain with Kenny talking him through the motions. The tall, thin Navajo, with his dark regular features and black hair tied in a neat bun behind his head, replied with an enthusiastic *"o'h', o'h'!"*—meaning "yes, yes!"

With Kenny praying that he would not pass out from the bouncing and jostling he was going to get, the nascent driver got behind the wheel, depressed the clutch, turned on the ignition, pressed the starter, and shifted into low gear. Once under way, Kenny decided to keep the truck in low gear, which would hold the speed down and thus reduce the stress on his body. After what seemed like an eternity of torture from the bouncing truck, they made it.

Even while Kenny, now partially recovered, was telling

me this remarkable saga, I realized I had never heard anything like it. I was struck by two things: Kenny had been able to use a language that had no words for many of the things the driver had to do and touch, and the Navajo seemed to have the capacity to look at this machine and visualize how it worked.

When Kenny would speak of his Navajo crews, his eyes would light up; though love was not an emotion a man in those days in the West would ever have admitted to out loud, I was sure that he loved them. From time to time, when the spirit moved him and he wanted to recall his experiences with his Navajo brothers, he would break out in song, reproducing as close an imitation as I have ever heard of the Navajos' Night Chant—a powerful falsetto yodel overlaid with frills and guts, a sound that sent shivers up and down my spine whenever I heard it.

So even before we first met, I had a feeling for The People, as the Navajos call themselves, as do many tribal people. The Navajo word is *Diné,* pronounced dee-nay approximately; it means "us"—"the people" as distinct from everyone else. The term, which I used and thought of often, had the connotation that we the people, *Diné,* were human and everyone else was not quite human. I saw nothing pejorative about this, because it had been axiomatic in anthropology that this was pretty much the way all groups thought of themselves. To introduce a note of relativism into our thinking: the term *Diné* is unlike American, Japanese, French, and other Indo-European appellations. Eventually, looking into such differences became my life's work. Having lived among the Navajo people and many others, I became convinced that the *Diné* represented one of the world's greatest unexplored and underutilized intellectual resources.

Greater than the difference between Homer's thought processes in *The Iliad* and those embedded in the script for "Star Trek," it is difficult to explain the differences in thinking between a culture such as the Navajo and our own. Such differences between peoples in their basic way of looking at the world and thinking about it, and uttering words about it, often appear as a kind of obstructionism, a stupid rebelliousness, a failure to "get it." We see this even among husbands and wives brought up in the same town. Imagine the confusion, anger, contempt, and anxiety among the Navajos when academicians as late as the early twentieth century, with their air of professional certainty, referred to them as "savages." For example, show someone of European culture something as simple as a color swatch—say, yellow—he or she will perceive the color yellow, perhaps even some describable shade of yellow, making a reference to an object such as the sun, which is also yellow. Show a Navajo the same color swatch and he or she will see a universe, the sun, a cardinal direction, geography, a class of minerals, a time of day, a body of historical lore, meaning, intent, a legion of Holy People, and more. And all of this implies also the three other cardinal directions, other colors, other classes of minerals, other stories, other meanings and intents—everything—as well as experiencing and conceiving the world comprehensively.

For a Navajo, the world is of a piece. Nothing can be seen by the Navajos (and by many other tribal peoples) as unconnected. Through such fields as ecology, the study of Eastern religions, quantum mechanics, and the teachings of my field—anthropology—we of European descent and thought patterns are only dimly edging toward an understanding of our part in the whole. To a Navajo, such an understanding is second nature, and we see it in their approach to the land. Like most American Indians I know anything about, they are tied to the land in a particular way. They do not see themselves as separate from nature but as part of it, whereas we tend to see nature as an array of forces to be conquered. "In the morning," one Navajo once told me, "the Navajo man, he gets up, he goes outside his hogan and turning to his right, he takes the end of a branch of the nearest juniper tree in his hand, and he says, 'Good morning, Grandfather,' and then he turns to his left and taking the pine needles at the end of a branch of a piñon tree in his hand, he says, 'Good morning, Grandmother.' In that way he reminds himself each day of his relationship to nature, of which he is a part. Everything in nature is sacred."

We have an adage that warns us about not seeing the forest for the trees. We may not see the forest for the owls, as well. Imagine that the "forest" is a series of unconnected, separate resources, like a supermarket that presents us with various categories of choices, each in its separate wrapper. To a Navajo, such thinking is insane, blind. To eat mutton, you have to butcher one of your sheep, spill its blood, which is not unlike your own.

Who are these people? It is a question I often asked myself while among them and after I spent those years with them west of the thirties. There were times on the reservation, particularly in winter, when I would have to pinch myself mentally to realize I was not in Outer Mongolia or even Tibet. I would be riding across an endless, depopulated plain when I would see horsemen on longhaired ponies—horsemen whose clothing, posture, faces, body-build, pattern of clustering their horses, all gave me the eerie impression of having been transported by some genie to the steppes of Mongolia on the other side of the globe.

It is not known precisely where the ancestors of today's Navajos arose. It is certain, however, that they were the most recent arrivals of the people we call Indians in North America, the last to cross the Bering Strait from Asia into Alaska. They were of a language stock we call Athapaskan. They penetrated the Arctic mostly along the coast—lands of the Eskimo—tarrying for some time in southern Alaska and northwestern Canada, where many of them still live today. But a few bands pushed southward through the Canadian woods, where the Algonquians settled, and kept moving along the great cordillera of the Rocky Mountains, ending up in the American Southwest.

They came, presumably, in small bands, no later than the early sixteenth century and perhaps a hundred or more years before the Spaniards began to press northward out of Mexico. An important, characteristic trait of the Navajos was their ability to selectively absorb customs and culture patterns, which were most useful, from other tribes—particularly from the Eskimos—they met on their way south. These Athapaskan-speaking people spread out in the hinterlands of a region occupied by more ancient village-dwelling agriculturalists, the Pueblo people—descendants of the Anasazi. One such loosely connected group of Athapaskans inhabited the area of northwestern New Mexico that surrounds what we call Gobernador Knob, a prominent peak near which the Navajos believe they emerged into this world. And they did. In the late 1930s, as an archeologist-dendrochronologist, my chief Hispanic assistant and I found the remains of a forked-stick type of hogan—something like a tepee made of logs. The piñon logs of the main supports dated to approximately 1540, suggesting that these people who would become known as the Navajos arrived in the Southwest not long before the Spanish.

When the Spanish arrived in the upper Rio Grande area in the 1540s, they learned from the Pueblo Indians that there were some people to the north and west who were different. Having already crossed paths with the southern Apaches, the Spanish named them *Apaches de Nabajó,* which loosely translated means the Apaches with knives— from the long stone knives they carried.

The Spanish had little to do with these northern neighbors when they found there was no gold to speak of in this new province. They focused instead on enslaving the more sedentary Pueblos and converting their souls to Christianity. After a hundred and forty years of subjugation by the Spanish, the Pueblo tribes decided that their bellies were full of the foul fare of the Spanish. One of their number, a strategist named Popé, traveled among his people, visiting every town—even the Hopis far to the west—leaving knotted cords at each pueblo with instructions to cut off one knot for each day. When the last knot was cut loose, they were to revolt and "kill all the Spanish in your village or on your lands." Impatiently the Indians waited. Then in 1680, the Pueblo Indians revolted, killing the priests and driving the Spanish out. A few, tipped off by Pueblo friends, escaped. But the Indians were smart enough to know that the Spanish would return, which they did, twelve years later in greater force and with greater determination.

With the return of the Spanish, many of the Pueblo people, fearing retribution, vanished, deserting their villages along the Rio Grande. No one knew where they went or what had happened to them. In fact, one of the great mysteries among the white people of the Southwest was where they had escaped to. The over two-hundred-year mystery was not solved until 1917 toward the end of World War I, when Alfred Vincent Kidder, the Southwestern archaeologist, traveling between Dulce and Aztec, New Mexico, noticed what looked like fortified towers a hundred or more feet above the Gobernador Wash. He made the arduous climb to the first of more than fifty such sites. There, nestled together in an easily defensible place, were the remains of Navajo hogans, Navajo pottery, and—of all things—Pueblo masonry dwellings and Pueblo potsherds. After all those years the refugee area had at last been found. The Pueblos had sought and found refuge with their Athapaskan neighbors whom we now know as the Navajos, living together in well-fortified sites that no persons in their right minds would attack in that rough and forbidding territory.

The Pueblo people, the ancestors of the Navajos, lived together, intermarried, shared technology, folklore, and crafts, and became the Navajo people. The full story of the results of this association has yet to be told, for there are bits and pieces of evidence that must be understood and identified before the puzzle is complete. We do know that the Navajos retained the essential Athapaskan language and the hogan, rather than the underground kiva, but they also practiced many Pueblo crafts such as polychrome pottery and weaving. And eventually, sometime in the eighteenth century they apparently moved west, having characteristically integrated some Pueblo traits but still returning to a more shamanistic emphasis in their ceremonial practices.

Still in the eighteenth century, Navajos who had occupied the country around Chinle and Canyon de Chelly were joined by various groups of Hopis fleeing drought conditions in their own mesa country at the southern edge of Black Mesa. The past of all these Southwestern tribes, seen as so distinct when set down in a few sentences of print, is nevertheless cluttered with cultural and genetic blurring as a consequence of these periods of cross-cultural emergence. The Indians seemed to be able to live with each other for a while and then would separate, having mixed their blood while still maintaining a kind of organic integrity. But a new and alien influence was to be introduced into their world by people who had a hierarchical approach to life and a low tolerance for differences.

As Europeans were colonizing the third world, they viewed the Indians who were on the land and their way of life as ignorant and obstacles to European progress. They found the common practice of raiding each other for food, livestock, and slaves—both male and female—at least on the surface intolerable. Raiding of this kind was common practice well into the nineteenth century. In fact, the desire for slaves on the part of the Spanish had the conquerors' seal of approval. By the time the United States took claim to the region in 1846, it is said thousands of Navajos, as well as other Indians, were slaves in Spanish homes.

The situation would have continued considerably longer if it had not been for General Stephen Kearny's U.S. Army, which occupied the former Mexican territory in 1846. Distracted by the approaching Civil War and not knowledgeable in the ways of the American Indian, the American government overreacted to raids by the Navajos. They didn't know that there were different bands and—typically, I might mention—thought that when they had an agreement with the leader of one band, they had reached an understanding with all the rest. The United States Army dispatched famed mountain man Colonel Kit Carson to round up the eight thousand Navajos and incarcerate them at a place called Fort Sumner (or Bosque Redondo), along the Pecos River in eastern New Mexico, where some five hundred Mescalero Apaches had already been interned.

Having lived in the country and driven, walked, and ridden on horseback and muleback over major portions of that immense and rugged land, I found it inconceivable that Colonel Carson could accomplish what he had set out to do—namely, rounding up Navajos, who were thinly scattered over 280,000 square miles of impassable terrain. The big question was "How did he do it?" As is frequently the case, the record was incomplete.

This question simply wouldn't let go, and I couldn't get it out of my mind. Then in the process of exploring the reservation, I picked up another mystery. This one made no sense at all. During the summer of 1935 I climbed Navajo Mountain, a sacred, dome-shaped peak eleven thousand feet in elevation, just north of the state line between Arizona and Utah and visible from most parts of the reservation. It was a long, arduous walk in the heat of August. But before long I had climbed into the cooler Hudsonian life zone characterized by Engelmann spruce and fir trees, a Canadian zone type of vegetation. There I discovered that the summit, a vast round area of several square miles, was covered with a dense aspen forest. Aspens, white-barked trees with flat-stemmed leaves that flutter in the wind, are pioneers. They occur after a heavy burn or a clear-cutting and over the years are usually squeezed out by the sturdy Engelmann spruce. Looking more closely, I could see that the ground was littered with the remains of felled spruce trees scattered higgledy-piggledy on all sides. These trees had not been felled by a windstorm nor had they been burned, because the branches were intact. A close examination of the stumps told me that the trees had been cut down with axes! It would have taken hundreds of men to fell a forest covering an estimated two thousand acres. I kept asking myself who could have inflicted such a capricious wound on the countryside, a task accomplished with no thought of gain or use of the timber. My mind was flooded with images. It was as though a bizarre, gargantuan, whimsical trick had been played by an insane billionaire, who had enough money to hire the hundred or more men to cut down all those trees in the most remote part of our country and having cleared the top of an entire mountain, picked up and left. Judging by the amount of bark left on the tree trunks as well as the growth of aspen, I estimated the job had been done more than fifty years before my visit and probably not less than sixty to seventy-five years. There were no traders in the country then; explorers like the Wetherill brothers would come later. "Navajo Mountain cleared as prank" is not an entry to be found in the index of a book.

A photograph of a soldier standing among newly cut timber in a book owned by Ben and John Wetherill provided the clue. Kit Carson had ordered that the summit be clear-cut, not for timber but to provide open space for a heliograph—a signaling device made with mirrors by which sunlight could be used to transmit coded messages over enormous distances. There had been heliographs as well at Fort Defiance and the eastern edge of the Grand Canyon. Whenever Carson's Ute trackers (among the best trackers in the West) found a concentration of Navajos, word would be transmitted quickly and the troops would arrive.

American servicemen incarcerated by the Vietnamese will have a feeling for the ensuing misery to which the

Navajos were subjected. The almost total devastation of their people was, and remains, the central event in the Navajo history of contact with the white man, leaving a scar to this day on the psyche of every Navajo. The "Long Walk" refers not just to the three-hundred-mile trek from Fort Defiance to Fort Sumner (with stragglers being picked off by slavers or even shot by the Army), but to the four years in Bosque Redondo. While the Navajos were interned at Bosque Redondo, an active attempt was made to destroy the Navajo lifestyle. Their food was handed out in inadequate stores of raw, uncooked flour, which they didn't know how to prepare. Potatoes, coffee, lard, and slabs of bacon were all unfamiliar. They were crowded together in a strange land in unsanitary conditions, suffering epidemics, living in pit houses, and told to become like Pueblo people. Some 10 percent died along the actual walk. In all, some eight thousand Navajos were rounded up, and four years later, when this lamentable experiment was declared a failure, only five thousand Navajos lived to return to their ancestral lands. Somehow they managed to retain their curing ceremonies, their sand paintings, their stories and legends of the past, their habits of relating and communicating, their social organization, and their language. In fact, they retained all the things the white man couldn't understand and at times even perceive. Once back in familiar territory, with a vitality bred from overcoming hardships, they rebounded with an astonishing vigor. From five thousand in 1868, the population had grown to fifty thousand when I was among them in the thirties. Today, after another sixty years, it is five times that. At about a quarter of a million, the Navajos are the largest Indian tribe on the North American continent, constituting nearly an eighth of all the native people in the United States.

During my prolonged stay on the reservation, my contact with the Navajos was mediated and enriched by the tutoring of mentors like Lorenzo Hubbell, my friend Ben Wetherill, and Sam Yazzie. It was not long before I began to get a feel for what the Navajos call *hozho,* beauty. This is the core of the Navajo world view. They have an English phrase—"walk in beauty"—but there is no apt English word for what they mean by beauty. It is both an aesthetic and an ethical concept, global in meaning, encompassing such attributes as congruence and harmony. It bespeaks the rightness of the creation. To fall out of congruence for whatever reason is to create disharmony and invite physical illness. All Navajo ceremonies, called sings, are curing ceremonies designed to restore beauty. The actual process of retelling in musical form the ancient stories of the Navajo creation (what we refer to as their mythology) acts to change the world and bring it back into harmony. For a Navajo, to speak is to act. They sing the world back into coherence, into being, into its original and emergent perfection.

The major ceremonies last from five to nine days (and nights) and cure the patient of a variety of ills caused by contact with outsiders, ghosts, witchcraft, lightning, and by violating a dizzying array of taboos (most of which, on examination, are intelligent and practical responses to living in the difficult countryside they inhabit). The sing is central to Navajo ceremonial life, all-inclusive, incorporating in one institution everything that Anglo culture allocates to almost a dozen separate institutions: healing, socializing, theater, visual art, music, recreation, sport, gambling, making love. The Navajos lived in widely separated locales, spending a good deal of time in small groups or alone out herding sheep. A sing was one of the few ways they could solidify their social bonds and, as we all must, re-reaffirm their culture. Presided over by one or more medicine men, a sing mobilizes great power—power to cure and power to harm if things are not done right. Every word of every "song" must be uttered in the right order and tone—every Navajo understands this—and *doing things right* is a potent factor in how the Navajo approaches any task, be it religious or practical (another distinction, by the way, the Navajos don't tend to make). Perceiving this, I began to see how it could have been that the Navajo crew could have so quickly mastered the art of driving an alien machine out of the woods and saving a broken white man's life. That driver had accurately recorded all the movements made by Kenny while he drove. All that was needed was the feeling in his muscles of being behind the wheel.

Even for someone who can't understand a single word of what is going on, to watch or to be involved in any way in a Navajo sing can be an overpowering event. The most dramatic, impressive, exotic experience of my life was the last night of a *Yeibichai* ceremony, the big night when the patient's family feeds all visiting participants. As noted, people throughout the region take part by attending with their minds, and when they can't be physically present, by mentally following the prayer plume as it is taken by the medicine men to distant sacred places. Feeding the people, providing gifts, and paying the medicine men—all make a sing expensive. Even in the thirties, a sing cost several thousand dollars and could consume the fortune of a wealthy Navajo family.

On the night of the Yeibichai I sat by a fire near the dancers' area, in front of the hogan in which the medicine man had made an elaborate sand painting and where he had sung over the patient during the day. I looked around at the firelit scene. Wagons had been pulled up in a U around the eastern side of the hogan, and the tongues of the wagons were tied up to make more room for the dancers. They seemed like ships' masts and rigging outlined against the black desert sky. Smoke rose from the central fire, sparks leaped in counterrhythm to the movements of the masked dancers. *Hoa ho! Hoa Ho! Hiiya hii.* I was immersed in the dance, the songs, the sound, light, shadow, and rhythm. I was overwhelmed by this different world, the pure energy of the ceremony, and a world I could only sense but never truly be a part of. Surprisingly, there was a joyousness I could feel without understanding.

A precious endowment of the Navajos is the ability to laugh, play, improvise, and simply live it up when they are together. During the day, when the curing is taking place inside the hogan, The People race their horses, gamble, and take pleasure in each other's company—as much sheer happiness as I have ever seen. Perhaps this is so pronounced because of the decidedly dark side of Navajo life —a dark side they meet directly. For the Navajo is confronted by a world ruled by danger, and evil is a tangible and aggressive presence in the world. When life leaves, death takes over, *chindi*, profoundly evil and dangerous— and terrifying. Werewolves and witches ubiquitously inhabited the shadows beyond the fire. Only fools (and witches) went abroad in the dark.

Lorenzo Hubbell once told me—with feelings of awe— of a Yeibichai when things went wrong. It was the fourth night of the ceremony. The wagons were drawn up around the entrance of the newly built earth lodge; fires crackled, providing warmth, light, and heat for cooking. All was going well. But suddenly, without warning a dark panther-like cloud enveloped the people and the ceremony; the singing stopped, chopped off as if by an axe. Silence—as though death had snuffed out all of life. In the distance a wolf howled, and the people shivered in terror. *The patient had died* and the *Diné* simply vanished into the dark.

Here were a people who had a powerful drive to be happy, but who lived under a shadow of immense density and magnitude. How was it, I wondered, that they were not simply overwhelmed. While I am not sure I will ever understand such things with anything approaching perfection, the question haunted me and drove me to look at my own culture, my own assumptions, those beliefs we hold that are out of awareness. Being human, we whites have a dark side as well, but we disassociate it, repress it, keep it out of our conscious awareness. The Navajos project it directly into the environment and must confront it squarely as it plays out its role, taming it temporarily through the continuing creativity of their search for *hozho* through their ceremonies.

Nowhere was this more evident than among the Navajo women, who were independent, with property and wills of their own. They were wonderful to watch as they strode about with a purposeful, vigorous, dominant gait evident through their pleated cotton Victorian skirts, which touched the ground. The leg was advanced sharply with a minimum of knee bend so that the heel came down hard while the toe was still pointed skyward—a gait like that associated in our culture with dominant males. These were powerful women. Each had her own account at the trading post, independent of her husband, and they were far tougher traders, drove harder bargains, and raised more hell when they thought things were not right.

They were by no means unfeminine, but they were

strong and tough, often a match for a man in a fight. Fights were not uncommon, usually arising from alcohol or infidelity. Once, when one of my crew failed to turn up on the job, I asked what had happened and was greeted with evasive humor. Later, I consulted Fletch at Lorenzo's trading post.

"Oh," said Fletch, "he had been carrying on with a woman below Oraibi near Teas Toh, and he lives over west of Dinnebito. He figured his wives wouldn't find out. Well, one of them was in here the other day and heard some women talking about it. He's in the hospital now. When he got home, his two wives were waiting. One had a pick handle and the other had a club. You wouldn't believe what they did to that man."

As a young white man, I was naturally curious about how other whites on the reservation handled sex. Those who slept with Navajo women often wound up marrying them. There were five white brothers from St. Michael's, a Catholic mission on the reservation, who married white women from Gallup and then, one by one, divorced their white wives and married Navajos.

I have from time to time speculated that one mechanism at work in such relationships may be the skin. Navajos share with many people whose origins are in Mongolia unusually soft skins, which I learned when I was helping out during a typhoid vaccination program. I couldn't get the texture of those skins out of my mind. When people are in love or strongly attracted, their skins tend to soften; when they are ill-disposed toward each other, the skin hardens. The message of the average Navajo's skin to a white person is a tacit message of love. Not having experienced the range of emotions as reflected in the Navajo skin, I simply cannot report how this particular communication system works in different circumstances.

As is found among all peoples of the world, a few Navajo women were notoriously free with their favors—though "free" is a misnomer; there was always a price. These women delighted in finding naive whites, such as new clerks in trading posts, to prey on. In one such instance, in Pinyon before the Hubbells owned the store, one of the new traders worked out an arrangement with a woman; they made love and she accepted the money, saying that everything was fine with her but that her husband might object. The trader remonstrated that he had made the arrangement with the woman, not with her husband. What was he supposed to do? She told him that he should buy a coat for her husband when he came into the store the next day. The clerk would know her husband because he would ask for a coat and mention his wife's name. The next day the woman was outside the store selling coats for ten dollars. All a man had to do was tell the trader he was the husband and that he had come to collect his coat. The young trader was said to have bought thirty-seven wool coats.

It was not difficult to see how white men got into trouble with Indian girls. Many of them were outrageously beautiful and sexy. According to the Hopis, if you had Navajo friends and slept outside their hogan, your chances of having sex were reasonably good because Navajo women were quite forward if they liked you. Despite an overactive libido, which would have kept me in hot water under ordinary circumstances, I never tried out the Hopi prescription. I was too inexperienced and shy, and everyone would have found out. I knew I couldn't get away with anything on the reservation. And I just couldn't see myself trying to work out a "date" in the middle of the trading post in a language I could barely speak. Furthermore, there was VD (sulfa was not known to the public). So I simply suffered and dreamed up fantasies of beautiful, seductive, willing Navajo girls.

Another Navajo distinction is in what psychologists call *affect*—feeling or emotion. Everything in Navajo culture, by virtue of their language, structures and adds coherence to what we, for want of a better word, call *mind*. Navajos have detailed and highly specific ways of thinking, acting, and perceiving. Not only are they highly visual and practical, but by eschewing the ideological in favor of a pragmatic realism, they place emphasis on the consequences of their acts without being sentimental or judgmental. In a word, they are less moralistic in the European sense than we are; this trait may have been picked up from the Eskimos.

Another contrasting side to Navajo psychology is one I have mentioned before—namely, that when things happen that disturb or disrupt harmony of mind, these events can take over and fill the entire area of consciousness. In such instances, a wrong can grow out of proportion to the act so that Navajos lose sight of the "consequences." The bright side of this dynamism (way of thinking and acting) as explained to me by Lorenzo is that an outsider can, by pointing out the consequences of their state of mind, use reason, gentleness, and persuasion to talk them out of a course of action that can lead only to disaster. He told me: *"They can kill, not for revenge but for peace of mind—a way of clearing the mind of an obsession."*

I had no trouble tracking the reality of what Lorenzo had said, but I could also see that others might ask, "How logical or realistic is it to think that killing a human being

has the same value as clearing one's mind of an obsession?" This is not easily explainable to most Westerners. It
will, however, give the Western reader a feel for the magnitude of the gulf separating our two cultures. In this sense it
would seem that the Navajo psychology, in the days when
I was familiar with it, had a deep stream of reachable realism that European and Arab cultures lack for different reasons. The Europeans and Arabs, at times and under certain
conditions, are willing to destroy themselves, and the
world too, for the sake of an idea or ideology.

When appraising the psychodynamic side of life, you
might say that the Navajos, once you get to know them,
are more up front than we are. It was this perception that
eventually made me see that it is the out-of-awareness,
tacit differences among us, which lie at the heart of the
tremendous misunderstandings that plague our species.

Another related characteristic, highly developed among
the Navajos but poorly understood in white society, is the
ability to be objective, to avoid the judgmental, the moralistic, and the ideological side of life. Of course, the Navajo
world view does include certain precepts, morals, taboos,
and other regulatory patterns and behaviors—most of
them elaborations on the practical needs for survival—but
they are more comfortable with life as a process, an ongoing series of events. White Americans always seem to put
some judgmental screen between themselves and the world
—ideological stances on such matters as population control, public health, poverty, justice, status, infidelity, sui-
cide, infanticide, euthanasia, costs, crime, drinking, smoking, gambling, religious beliefs, family values, social
responsibility, individual freedom. We personalize all such
matters via some ideologized judgmental screen or another. There is virtually no way we can talk about any of

our social institutions without invoking some implicit or explicit set of abstract *values,* some vital way in which we can disagree, set ourselves above others, and thus discredit them.

In their natural state all people are highly adaptable, but the Navajos seem to be among the most adaptable people on earth—not simply in adapting to new technologies (silversmithing, sheep raising, fixing the engine of a pickup, making computer components) but in their ability to live with, even absorb into their society, people who are different. People of European descent seem to be sorely lacking in this skill.

As a young man, I began to see how we white Americans may look to others. The Hopis experienced us as too fast, too intense, too individualistic, too tied to an abstract and artificial sense of time, not to mention too preoccupied with the idea of making them over in our own image. But to the Navajos, we must have seemed bland, unresponsive, wooden, not to mention a bit insane.

The Navajos struck me as a people with the capacity to consider with a high degree of objectivity the consequences of their acts without sinking into a moralistic and political morass. They had a vibrant sense of life, which we only occasionally attain. Resourceful in the bargain, they also loved to gamble. Both points are illustrated in the following story.

Gambling and horse racing were popular sports the Navajos thoroughly enjoyed. Joy in gambling was so characteristically Navajo, it quite obviously symbolized a pivotal center in their lives. To the missionaries, gambling had to be stamped out. It was like a proverbial red flag to the missionary bull. Although some missionaries were more obsessed with stamping out gambling than were others, one particular missionary in the Kayenta–Marsh Pass district became famous for the lengths to which he would go to combat this particular deadly sin. For him gambling was the Devil incarnate, an evil that must be tracked down and ruthlessly rooted out—vanquished at every turn. Whenever this benighted soul saw a circle of Navajo men kneeling on the ground, clearly intent on their game, his eyes would light up; putting spurs to his horse, he would gallop forth to break up the game, a practice that did not endear him to the Navajos. His lack of popular appeal naturally was ultimately reflected in the attendance at his church, which dwindled to a fraction of what it had been when he took over. Puzzling over what to do to boost attendance, he sent away for postcard-size Bible picture cards depicting Adam and Eve and the Serpent, the Annunciation, Jesus, the Holy Mother Mary, Joseph, the ride to Jerusalem on the donkey, Jesus' birth, the Sermon on the Mount, the Jews fleeing from Egypt, Moses in the bulrushes, and many other biblical incidents. The Bible cards worked like a charm and had the advantage of depicting the important facts in the development of Christianity. Because the cards were given away at the door to anyone attending the services, attendance boomed. The missionary was filled with the warm glow of success in doing God's work, a condition that persisted for several months. What was even more encouraging to him was that like the demon rum, gambling had vanished. He hadn't seen a game for months. But one day, while riding across the country looking for Navajos to convert, he approached an unusually large gathering of men kneeling in a circle, and they weren't praying. "They must be gambling. But why such a big crowd? I haven't seen a crowd like that before. Must be some kind of game I know nothing about." He was right about one thing; he didn't know anything about the game. The Navajos were so engrossed in their game that they had failed to post the usual scout to warn the players that the Enemy of Gambling was approaching. It wasn't just that he had been breaking up their games, causing all sorts of confusion with money and cards scattered all over the place, but for another reason. Navajos abhorred confrontations. And they felt they had enough trouble in their lives without having to put up with being berated by a raving maniac every time they got together to enjoy themselves. All his yelling and screaming scared them because people who act like that could only be demented.

Spurring his horse forward, the Enemy of Gambling arrived unnoticed because of the complete absorption of the players. Wanting to know the size of the pot on the blanket, which he habitually stole for his church, he stood up in his stirrups and with hands on the swell of the saddle, leaned forward to get a better view of the game. Looking down, he was just in time to see one enthusiastic player trump Joseph with the Holy Mother! The Navajos by then had managed to acquire a complete set and had invented an incredible, marvelously complex game with the Sunday school cards.

I couldn't help but speculate at some length on the stories I had heard about the supernatural. I couldn't just dismiss them because here all around me were people who literally inhabited another world. I would ask myself questions such as what it must be like to be "knocked up by an owl," a tale told to Lorenzo by a terrified Indian who had come seeking refuge one night. The man told Lorenzo he didn't feel safe with that owl flying around out there. When Lorenzo told me about it, his eyes flashed while he talked.

There had been a loud, continuous pounding on the door one night, the kind that wouldn't go away. When Lorenzo opened the door, a half-crazed Navajo man stumbled in, terror in his eyes, announcing *Besh Begoa* (Gold Tooth) had been knocked up by an owl. I never did get the whole story of what this was all about, but I assumed that the owl was a witch who was on the loose, and the messenger was afraid of the same fate. The imagery, however, is something I had trouble integrating. Leda and the swan, OK, but a man and an owl was another order of reality, and a pregnant male was more than I could integrate. Werewolves were in my own tradition and the very idea scared me. Living on the reservation, I learned enough to take the magic seriously, for to be bewitched could be fatal. Two white men I knew lost their lives this way. I wondered what it was like to live with overwhelmingly powerful forces, which must be guarded against and kept in harmony with one another as well as with human beings. The Navajos, like ourselves, build their lives on the assumption that there is order in the universe and that one must live in harmony with that order. However, I also knew that their order was different from mine. They inhabited a world where time was not linear and irreversible but was like a disk going off in all directions, so that the "future" as we know it was not ahead but was all around. What was it like to live a life of commitments and bargains but with no ironbound rules of logic in the white man's sense? Where logic seemed to be a low-context way of thinking something the white man dreamed up to confuse the minds of the Navajos, and a world where there were no technical Navajo laws but a white man's law, which only the white man's lawyers understood. What would it be like to live where so much was known about the forces controlling life that one had to be watchful and meticulous not just in some things but in all things? Where beauty and harmony must be in all things and are the primary values? Where there was total involvement within and between humanity, nature, and the supernatural?

I began to realize I lived in a world and acted according to the dictates of a legal system I did not understand because they were in the hands of specialists who complicated them to the point of inaccessibility to the average person. I asked myself how I could possibly place myself above these people, as most whites did, when I didn't even understand the most obvious controls of my own world.

For all the woes of their history, for all the palpable dangers and evils they faced each day, the Navajos did indeed walk in beauty in a haunted, challenging land of stark Manichaean harmony. It is hard to explain, but I know truly, though inadvertently, that they sang *me* into being. And I might well have missed the message had it not been for my friend Lorenzo Hubbell.

8

The Government
in Sheep's Clothing

. . . . "Is that the reason so many tea-things are put out
here?" she asked.

"Yes, that's it," said the Hatter with a sigh: "it's always
tea-time, and we've no time to wash the things between
whiles."

"Then you keep moving round, I suppose?" said Alice.

"Exactly so," said the Hatter: "as the things get used
up."

"But what happens when you come to the beginning
again?" Alice ventured to ask.

"Suppose we change the subject," the March Hare inter-rupted, yawning. "I'm getting tired of this. . . ."

—LEWIS CARROLL, *Alice's Adventures in Wonderland*

ONE OF THE SPINOFFS of FDR's New Deal, the Soil Conservation Service (SCS), a division of the Department of Agriculture, had been created to solve the Dust Bowl problem of the thirties. Out of the blue in fall 1933, the Soil Conservation Service burst into our small world.

To add to the woes of the Great Depression, a period of widespread and prolonged drought had occurred. The people farming the High Plains were starkly and suddenly faced with the consequences of a half century of profligate use of the former tallgrass prairie lands: deep plowing in straight rows without regard to contours or erosion, minimal if any attention to the benefits of crop rotation, and no fallow periods in which the land was given time to recover. They had exploited the soil of one farm and then, when productivity waned, moved on. It was standard practice in the West. The farmers took no heed of the first small dust storms that blew up in the twenties. Then, in the depth of the depression, the big ones hit. Drought and high winds produced dust storms of unimaginable magnitude; topsoil of the Western High Plains became airborne, turning the sky opaque for days and weeks at a time. Some of the dust settled on the streets of New York City and on the desks of New Dealers in the nation's capital. The storms were so powerful and intense that we commonly saw automobiles arriving in Santa Fe with paint sandblasted from one side and with the driver sticking his head out the other side in order to see, because the sand had frosted the windshield.

On a trip to Denver, I had to replace an entire motor because dust had penetrated the filters. So the Soil Conservation Service came into being.

Early on in the SCS experience came stories about how hard it was to explain to farmers the need to change their methods. One of the SCS men told me about a farmer who exclaimed, "Hell, man! You can't tell me anything about erosion. Me and me old lady have worn out three farms already." Many farmers simply didn't seem able to grasp the cause and effect of erosion on their land. Another extension agent in desperation wrote Washington, asking for a thousand pictures of the Grand Canyon to illustrate his point. For a long time it seemed that erosion and the depression were the only things we in the West could talk or think about.

It was soon apparent that with all their sincerity, technical competence, idealism, and identification with a good cause, the SCS men were butting their heads against a stone wall labeled resistance to change. The SCS had to learn to communicate to farmers in a language they could respond to. The well-meaning experts just didn't know how to talk to farmers. Sociologists at the Department of Agriculture spent a good deal of time researching these communication difficulties, but something important was still missing. Eventually, with the sociologists' help, the SCS learned and in the process were able to make great strides in overcoming the bugaboo of new ideas. In the High Plains states, where the major damage was being done, shelterbelts of trees were planted to reduce the wind, and contour plowing was instituted to reduce erosion. The story is one of the great successes in applied social science, the telling of which is another tale in itself. Having learned about the hidden fears of farmers, many (but not all) as-

sumed that these hidden rules gleaned after extensive research on how to communicate with white farmers were
universal and equally applicable to everyone. They were,
of course, dead wrong.

My own experience with the SCS and the Navajos, with
the Dust Bowl of the Plains looming in the background,
was akin to being on the edge of a tremendous hurricane.
Big things were going on around the eye of the storm—
frantic efforts to save America's soil *and* soul. Then suddenly I was part of a runaway process, a kind of stampede
utterly out of control. In fall 1933 we got a message that
all our work was being shut down and that instructions
would follow later. It was the time of year when lambs
were growing to marketable size, and the Indians would
soon be bringing them in to sell to the traders, and paying
off some of their debt.

The ECW personnel from the Hopi Reservation were
instructed to drive the 195 miles from Keams to Tuba City
in the westernmost part of the Navajo Reservation. We sat
like schoolchildren on folding chairs on the basketball
court of the Indian school and listened to the SCS tell us
that Washington had decided to reduce the herds of Navajo sheep. For a decade or so there had been official fret-
ting and hand-wringing that Navajo herds were degrading
the land. Their point to us now was that there were not
only too many sheep but too many old sheep with no teeth
pulling up the grass and as a result overgrazing the land.
They said we were temporarily being drafted into the SCS
to buy sheep from the Navajos. In each district the
Navajos were instructed to bring their sheep to a designated spot where the weeding out would take place. Nothing was said about what was to be done with the sheep
except that they would be trucked off the reservation. We

were told to buy only "gummers and shells" (an apt description) with few or no teeth. The implication was that they would be sold to the makers of chicken feed and the like.

The Soil Conservation Service men were like highly dedicated missionaries, but instead of saving sinners and heathens, they were out to save the soil. As technicians, they knew their trade, but the truth was they didn't know all there was to know. Convinced that their cause was just, that God was on their side, and that they really did know all there was to know, they couldn't be stopped. No field study had been done to demonstrate that reducing the sheep population would have a beneficial effect on the reservation range, but like all bureaucrats with a good cause and with the government's power, money, and technical knowledge behind them, they kept pushing their own version of common sense. According to our own Western way of thinking, on the surface their logic was unassailable.

The Indians did not see it that way. Laws, logic, and technical approaches to soil conservation developed to cope with the people, as well as with the conditions found in the High Plains, simply did not apply to the high, dry mesa country of the Navajos and the Hopis. Yes, the soil was dry and it was eroding but not, as they insisted, because of overgrazing. Drought had occurred before and was cyclical in nature.

The dry cycle on the reservation had started at the beginning of this century. Before that, the dry arroyos and washes so familiar to those of us born in this century weren't there; they were caused by a change in the climate, a drought that began before the 1930s when the population densities of Navajos and sheep were significantly lower. The sheep didn't help the situation, but they weren't the cause, either. The cause was drought—a far longer drought than that which afflicted the Plains like a sudden eruption of God's wrath. The Navajos didn't like what was happening. Since the beginning of the eighteenth century, their economy had been deeply rooted in herding sheep. The sheep provided food as well as wool for spinning into yarn and dyeing and weaving into blankets and rugs, which were sold at the big-city markets via the traders.

At the first meeting in Tuba, a distinguished old Navajo man stood up on the stage. I can still see him in my mind's eye: tall, eloquent, truthful. He spoke in his native tongue through an interpreter, but the interpreter was not really necessary. His gestures told why he felt the way he did. He detailed dramatically how each year he harvested wool and a lamb from each of his ewes, and at the end of the year he still had the ewes. But if the government paid him money and took his ewes, the money would not be there at the end of the year. His gestures showed how the money would sift like burning hot sand through his fingers. First facing right with outstretched hands in the act of receiving the money in his upturned palms, he then turned and faced left, and while he turned, the money drained away. As he turned, time shrank and you could almost see the money vanishing. Then he turned again, stretching out his hands for the money. This time he put the money in his pocket, but the pocket had a hole in it and the money was lost.

To the SCS, issues were simple and clear-cut—too many sheep and not enough grass. Any fool could see that. And any fool could see the logic: when the grass is scarce from overgrazing, the quality of the sheep's wool deteriorates, which means that it doesn't bring as high a price on the wool market as it would when the range has not been overgrazed. If the Navajos will reduce their herds now, in a few years the range will recover, and with a proper range-control program the sheep will again produce high-quality wool, which will sell on the Boston wool market for enough to make up the difference between the loss of income sustained as a result of selling their sheep to the government. Then there was another point to remember. When the government reduces the number of Navajo sheep, they will, in the process, improve the herd by weeding out the old sheep—the gummers and the shells, which pull up the grass by the roots.

Their logic was unassailable *provided* you were used to an Aristotelian paradigm and accepted the assumptions that logic was based on. Not only were their assumptions wrong on several scores, but as I had learned from my own futile efforts to "reason" with my own crews, our carefully prepared linear arguments simply made the Indians anxious. You might ask, why did our logic make the Navajos anxious? Just look at the discussions about how American men and women misunderstand each other by misperceiving the underlying logic of an argument, and any time you have trouble following someone else's reasoning; the results are out-and-out rejection, withdrawal, or anxiety.

A further complication in the sheep-reduction program centered around those of us who were actually going to have to buy the sheep. We knew what the Navajos used them for. Driving around as we did, we would pass grazing herds daily. We had eaten mutton, bought wool blankets from women who had spun and dyed their wool. We knew all the byproducts and something about the people around the sheep. But we didn't know sheep as sheep.

There would be times when I would pass a young shepherd—six or eight years old—with his or her head barely visible above the backs of a herd of grazing sheep. How was it possible to herd sheep as a part of the herd? It was the Navajos' *relationship* to their sheep that enabled the six-year-old Navajo child to stand in the middle of the herd without scattering the sheep. I found this to be extraordinary. The sheep and the people reacted to each other as though they were the same species! Normally, sheep will run from someone who approaches them. Having been around animals most of my life, I could see that the sheep not only were not afraid of their owners but were actually comfortable with them, the way some people and horses are. In retrospect, I can see that the young Navajos were actually *imprinted* on the sheep and vice versa, in much the same way the German ethologist Konrad Lorenz's goslings were imprinted on him. For a moment, try to imagine what it would be like to be in the middle of a herd of animals that come up to your shoulders and to be immersed in the strong smell of their wool and comforted by the baas coming from all directions as mothers and lambs keep in touch. And in addition, you hear the gentle crunch of grass being eaten and the patter of hooves on the soft Western soil as each sheep moves forward to the next clump of grass. Consider what it would be like to know all the sheep individually, with some your friends, as a person can be friends with a horse. Then you will begin to experience the way the Navajos felt about their sheep. As the old Navajo headman said, money burned his hands and he couldn't hold on to it. What we whites did not understand was that although the Indians didn't love their money the way we do, they did love their sheep.

Sheep and money were not interchangeable. Sheep were not a commodity as they were for us. Each sheep was known individually. Any Navajo with a herd could tell you how many lambs each ewe had dropped and could identify every lamb's mother. There was an ongoing relationship between the herd's owner and every sheep in the herd, which was why a Navajo shepherd could walk out into the middle of the herd, pick out a sheep, and carry it away without scattering the rest of the herd.

Lorenzo had told me, "When a little girl is able to walk, they take her out into the middle of the herd, and she puts her arms around the neck of a ewe lamb. That lamb will be the beginning of *her* herd. All the sheep springing from that one ewe belong to that little girl." I saw confirmation of this one time when I needed a sheepskin to put on the floor next to my cot and stopped by a hogan to buy one. After I selected a particularly soft dark hide, the Indians had me give the money for the hide to a little girl who couldn't have been more than three and a half. It had come from her herd.

Not only did the Navajos love their sheep, but they thought of them as members of the family just as we think of a dog we love as part of the family. When an old ewe had dropped so many lambs and had been shorn of her wool an equal number of times, it didn't matter that her wool was of inferior quality because her badly worn or nonexistent front teeth made it impossible for her to get enough to eat. It didn't matter that she was no longer round, filled-out, and firm, or that she was so thin her body sank in at the sides. She had a right to live because she had produced so much. The family was not about to sell her just because some white man thought that by selling her, they would "improve" the herd.

Beyond that (in fact, very much a part of that) was the very real Navajo psychology of time, the importance of the present in their lives, and an added dimension to the basic misunderstanding being unleashed on the reservation. In those days only the rare white person knew that there was such a thing as Navajo or Hopi culture in the sense that it is known today. But recognized or not, it was there. According to Lorenzo, promises of future benefits meant virtually nothing to the Navajo Indian. You could be the owner of the most beautiful horse on the reservation—a horse that won races against all the other horses, a horse that an Indian would give anything to have. You knew he dreamed about that horse. But should you say to that Navajo that since he has been such a good friend and worked so hard, this time next year—if he continued to perform as he had—you would reward him by giving him the horse, he would turn on his heels and walk away; the promise of future rewards is meaningless to him.

On the other hand, if you were to say to him, "Did you see that horse *Klizi Klani* (Many Goats) just rode up on? He's tying it up to the hitching rack right now. Look at him. He's just come off the range and he's a little thin, the saddle is old and worn just like the saddle blanket on the horse's back. Well, I own that horse. And because you are my friend, and because you have done so well, I want to give you something. Take that horse, he's yours. Do what you want with him. You can have the saddle and bridle, too. And take the saddle blanket." Then that man's chest will swell with joy and pride and he won't be able to wait to get to the hitching rail, get on that horse, pull the reins tight, turn his head while setting spurs to his flank, and ride off.

Though future rewards meant nothing to the Navajos, the SCS was building its whole strategy of persuasion around a logic of future rewards, which were complete and utter non sequiturs when placed in the context of Navajo culture. Talk like that didn't make sense to the Navajos, so they were anxious. The Navajos had learned from past experience that whenever the white man talked crazy like that, something valuable was about to be taken away from them. The Navajos knew about the cycles of wet and dry years in their part of the country. They knew when the erosion had started and that it was caused by the drought, which had reduced ground cover. Also, they knew that until the rains came, there was nothing to hold the soil and that if the weather were to change, it would not be because of some government program to take away their sheep. But how were they to explain all these things to the white man?

All this was much on their minds when the Navajos started driving their sheep to designated spots such as Hard Rock Crossing on the Oraibi Wash southwest of Pinyon, where we were posted. We knew almost nothing about the age cycle of sheep, and no matter how hard we tried, it would have been impossible to carry out the government's intentions to buy only those old sheep doing the most damage to the range. We couldn't distinguish between a big lamb just getting its teeth and an old ewe losing its teeth.

The test the experts used was to hold the sheep's mouth open and snatch a quick look. There is only a fraction of a second where the head is at the right angle and the mouth opens wide enough with the tongue out of the way so that you can get a good look at the teeth. If you didn't know exactly what you were looking for in that half-open, straining, bobbing jaw (while you're trying to remember what someone standing on a stage two weeks ago had told you), the chances of making a mistake were about three out of four. The inside of a sheep's mouth was as familiar to us as a Ming Dynasty vase.

We might have done better if the SCS people had given us an orientation session with real sheep. They could even have butchered a few sheep and passed the heads around for us to examine at our leisure. But the SCS people didn't know how little *they* knew and how little *we* knew and how ignorant we both were about what we needed to know to do the job right. All they could say was, "Be sure you don't buy any lambs—buy shells and gummers but not lambs." No one told the SCS that the Navajos would much rather sell a young sheep, which had yet to become a member of the family, than a beloved old aunty whose sides were caving in. Nor would they have believed it if the Navajo had said as much.

When the time arrived, the process of buying the sheep proved to be nothing less than mass confusion. The herds converged on Hard Rock Crossing (now called Hard Rocks, where there is a chapter house—a sort of regional headquarters in the Navajo Nation). Several of us were detailed to do the paperwork as well as examine the sheep as they were brought in one by one by their owners. It was a nightmare. Thirsty sheep on all sides pushed toward the water in a small hollow in the rocks. It was a miracle that anything worked at all, with ovine chaos and panic and human chaos and panic. From dawn through dusk without a break, the world was madness. Then it was over. But such an experience is never over. It haunts me now, more than a half century later, and it still haunts the Navajos even more profoundly.

The reduction program took on an even more brutal form elsewhere later on. Government agents would simply show up at a Navajo camp and shoot down the requisite number of sheep as the family watched helplessly. The point of the program was never explained to these isolated people on the reservation. The Navajos blamed the sheep-reduction program on John Collier, and it is still remembered by the Navajos as the most devastating treatment they received in their history outside of the Long Walk.

Possibly because the SCS personnel were afraid of what the results might be, they made no publicized attempt to evaluate the social impact of the program or to determine whether, after all this devastation, any positive results had been achieved. Many of us, according to what the Navajos told us, had bought lambs instead of shells and gummers, and all I could think of was those nice fat lambs being turned into chicken feed. Through our own ignorance we probably ended up leaving more shells and gummers than lambs on the range—creating the opposite effect than was planned by the experts, which was fewer old ones, better grass, better wool. It was clear the Indians knew what was going on, because one of the ECW staff got his Navajo name in the course of the reduction. They called him *Tepe Yazzie,* or Little Lamb, because he bought so many lambs. This said as much about Navajo humor as it did about the program. *Tepe Yazzie* became a metaphor for government and how it works, but I suppose we were all part of the metaphor.

It was a sorry time. Nor had it been the first offense visited on the Navajos in the name of range control. Only a few years earlier, Navajo horses had been rounded up and slaughtered. As for the Plains Indians, the Navajo Indian and his horse were made for each other, enjoying a kind of psychic unity. In the history books nothing much has been made of the horse-reduction program. It occurred in the mid-twenties, less than ten years before my arrival on the reservation. At that time, you will recall, the Indians were still treated as children and they were still legally minors.

The Navajo horse was evidently a much diluted but still spirited remnant of the Spanish conquest horse in North America, specially bred for stamina and speed—a cross between an Arab and a Barb. The government's excuse had been that the horses had dourine, a relative of syphilis and supposedly a disease to which the Arabian horse is prone. But the argument at the time was that the horses were not economically productive and that they should be replaced by sheep! What the government officials really objected to was that some Navajos owned as many as one hundred to one hundred fifty horses. A Navajo's status was linked to, among other things, the size of his horse herd, and they just couldn't stand the idea of an Indian's having one hundred or more horses as status symbols. This stuck in the bureaucratic craw like a bone lodged crosswise.

A friend, Will J. Barker, a federal judge in Santa Fe, told me, "The least they could have done was to strike some medals saying Fifty-Horse Man, Hundred-Horse Man, and the like and given them to the men whose horses were taken. It would have made sense and been more humane. As it was, the Indians were left with nothing."

As with the sheep, there was another and vindictive side to the horse reduction, which I learned from Lorenzo one night when he described the annual July fourth celebration and roundup in Flagstaff. Each day there would be horse races, and the Navajos would bet and lose while the white ranchers were winning. The Navajos didn't have stopwatches. They didn't need them, because they knew the relative speed of every horse entered in the previous races at Flagstaff and carried this information in their heads. The first three days of racing were devoted to research on the relative speed of the white ranchers' horses, first to each other, then to the Navajo horses. The last day was inevitably a shoo-in because the Navajos held their fastest horse in reserve. Then on the last day came the big race and the big purse, and the Navajos would enter one of their Arab-Barb champions. By then, the cowboys were so used to the Navajos losing that they were willing to take some big-money bets. The Navajo strategy always seemed to work until the white man's government killed off the Navajos' best horses.

The year following the sheep reduction, a remarkable man turned up at Lorenzo's. A tall and relaxed individual with the breath of the outdoors about him, Dr. Young-blood had enthusiasm coupled with an inquiring scientific mind that looks for new solutions to old problems. He was a geneticist, employed by the Department of Agriculture, committed to doing something to bring in more money to the reservation economy.

Repeated attempts to upgrade the Navajo wool by intro-ducing high-grade wool produced from foreign sheep, like the hardy French Rambouillet, had inevitably ended with the same results: the fine wool degraded as soon as the sheep had to survive on the meager fare provided by the Navajo range. According to Youngblood, the real problem with the Navajo sheep was not the poor fodder of our dry ranges but in the *relationship* of the sheep to the range. Instead of raising imported breeds on poor range, his plan was to develop a breed of indigenous sheep selected from ones already producing wool with the precious, fine long-staple fibers, which brought high prices on the Boston wool market. He had demonstrated that such sheep existed on the reservation, but there were not enough of them. He estimated that if things went well, the basic herd could be started in five to seven years and that in twenty years all the Navajo sheep would comprise this new indigenous breed.

Dr. Youngblood showed me photographs of greatly enlarged cross sections of wool fibers, taken of thinly sliced samples embedded in wax so that the cross sections could be analyzed, measured, and graded under a microscope. He explained that the method was new and made possible by an entirely new way of grading and ultimately classifying wool not only from different sheep but from different parts of a single sheep. Until then, measuring the wool meant measuring each fiber with a caliper—a painfully slow, laborious process that not only failed to yield information concerning the *shape* of the wool fibers but did not provide other important information either—for example, the proportion of thick fibers to thin fibers. A herd was actually started at Fort Defiance, New Mexico, but World War II bureaucracy and politics intervened before Youngblood's plan could be carried to its logical conclusion.

Observing both sides of the sheep-reduction program raised serious doubts in my mind about what happens when people or governments rush into things without taking time to assess the consequences. Equally important was the problem of interfering in other people's lives with insufficient information about the people themselves. None of this was difficult to see once it was known and accepted that American Indians were not just underdeveloped white men and women but the unique product of a complex, highly sophisticated, rational system of life. They were in many ways better adapted to their environment than we were to ours. What I now knew, having absorbed more and more of the reservation culture, was that one person's logic can end up as another's insanity. This conflict of two different kinds of logic was illustrated by an Arab folktale

attributed to Kahlil Gibran, which my father told me as a
boy of eleven.

Every day the people of the kingdom would come to the
well and drink of its water. One night the witch of knowledge
poisoned the well with a magic potion so that anyone drinking from the well became "insane." The next day the people
came, and drawing water from the well, quenched their thirst.
That evening when the desert air had cooled, the king and his
court went to the well and drank. The next morning there was
great rejoicing among the people, because the king and his
court had regained their sanity.

9

The Trading Business

IN 1933 THE TRADING POST was the economic core of reservation life, as well as the frontline defense against starvation for many Indians when times were hard. The relationship between the trader and the Indians who were his customers was symbiotic—neither could have survived without the other.

The early trading posts, dating back to the end of the last century, were purely utilitarian structures. Lorenzo's store was built at a time when traders felt the need to protect themselves from drunken and at times violent customers. Entering, you went from the blinding glare and stifling heat of the desert into the cool and dark interior of the trading post. After your eyes adjusted, you found a visual feast. All manner of tack and other goods hung from the vigas (logs used as roof beams), and what light there was came from a couple of small barred windows about ten feet above the ground, high enough to discourage break-ins. The only other space that left me with a similar visual feeling was years later when I visited Le Corbusier's magnificent chapel at Ronchamp. Naturally, the early trading post was diminutive in scale and lacked Corbusier's touch, but the effect was still evocative (there is no term in the English language to express that amalgam of visual and emotional responses elicited by certain architectural spaces). Counters were chest-high on a small man and undercut so that it was possible to rest your folded arms horizontally on the counter as though it were a wide mantelpiece. The effect, although comfortable, was to reduce your psychological height to that of a child. The trader, meanwhile, stood on a raised platform behind the counter like a parent or a king surveying his subjects below. When he put his hands on the counter, he had to lean over and look down at you from twenty inches above. This design feature, common to most trading posts of the time, grew out of necessity. Drunks are drunks, no matter where you find them in the world, and if there was no one to protect you, you protected yourself as best you could.

As in the rest of the country, there was little or no cash on the reservation during the Great Depression. Most Indians were in hock to the trader because although many produced either silver jewelry or blankets, the return was insufficient to maintain a family. Blankets, for example, were bought and sold to retailers by the pound! Fifty cents a pound for an ordinary (thick) blanket; one dollar a pound for a good blanket, well woven with even edges; and one dollar and fifty cents for an especially well woven, thin blanket. A good blanket that would go for twenty or twenty-five dollars then would sell on today's market in the low-five-figure range. Because prices for lambs and wool fluctuated and many Navajos did not raise sheep, there was simply no way for most Navajos to get ahead of the game and be independent of the trader. As a consequence, neither the Indians nor the traders were free agents.

Technically, the Indians were "wards of the government," which meant that the traders had to work within a tight set of regulations allowing little leeway in how they did business. For example, apart from buying lambs and wool, traders were forbidden from doing business away from their trading posts. All the traders were servicing huge debts to the banks and moneylenders because it was necessary to carry their customers from one lambing season and one shearing season to the next. Credit limits for the Indians were set in terms of the size of an individual's herds and of what are now referred to as futures in lambs and wool. When the price of either fell short, the trader was left holding the bag. There were always bad debts—Indians who didn't pay—exacerbated by traders who would extend credit to an Indian, knowing full well that he was already in hock to another trader. Stores were robbed and pawned jewelry was stolen. Insurance rates, when insurance was available at all, were high, as was interest on money needed to carry a trader from one lambing season to the next.

Possibly because their prices for all items were double or more than those for similar goods in town, Indian traders had a reputation among whites for skinning the Indians. Ten-cent sardine cans were twenty cents. A nickel box of soda crackers was ten cents. A fifteen-cent can of tomatoes was thirty cents. Gasoline was even worse: standard gas selling for twenty-five to thirty cents a gallon on the railroad was eighty cents to a dollar on the reservation. Given the roads and the distances that gasoline trucks had to travel, it was a minor miracle that any gasoline at all found its way onto the reservation. Indeed, the pumps frequently did run dry. Most of us not only carried extra gas in cans but carefully planned our travel around the location of gas pumps. I knew the location of every gas pump within a ninety-mile radius of Oraibi. Prices on the reservation were high, just as they are on virtually any island, but almost without exception the traders I knew were honest, typically struggling to keep their heads above water.

Another hidden cost of doing business on the reservation was due to the poor quality of the range; lambs and cattle bought from the Indians had to be fattened at the feedlot by operators, who could not care less about the effect of their sharp practices on the trader. The end result was that without an extensive network of stores supporting each other. And even with substantial financial backing—regardless of how savvy the trader was—trading was an extremely risky business. As one of them said to me, "How many rich traders do you know of?" There were some rich Indians like Chee Dodge, a Navajo headman and acknowledged leader of the tribe in the twenties, who was said to have had a herd of fifty thousand sheep, which would have made him a wealthy man indeed. I used to know his son, Tom Dodge, when he lived in Santa Fe.

The trading post had its own tempo. Possibly because of the low light level, most trading posts were pervaded by an atmosphere of quiet, verging on the depressive. Entering for the first time, you were struck by the virtually total absence of movement. In American hillbilly country stores, such stillness would have been a reliable cue not to start anything and to be especially careful about what you said. In the Navajo context, the message was different. Remaining engaged in their own transactions, Navajo women seldom even turned around when someone entered the post. All you saw was a broad expanse of behind covered by a pleated Navajo skirt, topped by the outline of a strong back and a head of straight black hair tied in a bun at the back. This lack of response was hard on white newcomers to the reservation, particularly those from the big Eastern cities who burst into a store expecting everyone to reassure them by immediately acknowledging their presence and the validity of their needs. I soon acquired the habit of opening the door quietly in the Navajo way, squeezing in sideways so as not to let in too much light or disturb the air, and waiting for the proper amount of time for people to get used to my presence. I let the trader—when he was ready— ask me where I had come from. It was in this context, whenever I was working with another culture, that I first acquired the habit of letting others set the tempo as well as the order of events. It is the only way to avoid some of the more flagrant errors in intercultural relations.

It could take thirty minutes to an hour just to find out whether the road through Blue Canyon from Red Lake to Oraibi was passable or not. Other whites in the car outside seldom understood what was taking so long, and tired of waiting, they would come to see what was holding me up. They would open the store door wide, stamp their feet, and raise their voices with a nerve-shattering effect.

"Oh, there you are. I wondered what was taking you so long. Say, this place is kind of dark, isn't it?"

For the traders' relationships with each other, distances

were great, competition real, resources scarce, and communication difficult and fragile. Yet every trader knew most of
what was happening on the reservation. There were three
sets of basic alliances: traders underwritten by Babbitt &
Company, a northern Arizona mercantile group with powerful political and commercial connections; the Lee outfit,
who were Mormons aggressively in search of a niche; and
Lorenzo Hubbell's chain of a dozen posts. Each group was
characterized by its own trading style, set by the man at the
top. Lorenzo's posts were geared more to the culture and
buying habits of the Navajos. The Babbitt posts, like the
one at Jeddito, were conservative, not aggressive, and run
from the point of view of the white man's business world.
The Mormon traders had a reputation for being more aggressive in their business practices. Here and there, independent traders like the Wetherills of Kayenta, Slim Halderman at Keams, and the well-known Lippincotts at Wide
Ruins, south of Ganado, eked out a living without the support and backing of a larger organization and were not
aligned with any group.

The Babbitt group was and still is a powerful, influential
component in the circles that run Arizona (Bruce Babbitt
was governor of the state in the 1980s). The Lee group was
tied to equally influential and cohesive forces in Salt Lake
City and Washington, D.C. The Spanish side of the Hubbells had been in the country since the time of the Spanish
conquistadores. During my years on the reservation, I
never heard anything derogatory about any of the Babbitt
traders. In fact, they were so low-profile that you had to
know something about the trading business to know that
the Babbitt family was involved at all.

The most recent and the most aggressive was the Lee
outfit. They had a reputation among other traders for be-

ing more than casual with regulations both written and unwritten concerning what was and what was not to be done in the trading business. One of the Babbitt traders, Chi Roberts in Jeddito, south of Keams, told me about Indians who had been co-opted in his area by the nearby Lee trader. The Spanish side of the Hubbell family had once owned vast stretches of land west of Albuquerque and was also politically strong at the grassroots level in Apache County during the territorial period. Lorenzo Hubbell, like his father, J. L. Hubbell, was politically adept and spoke Navajo before he spoke English, which set him apart from the other traders. Like Lorenzo, another friend of mine, Ben Wetherill, was allied biculturally, morally, intellectually, and emotionally with the Indians.

Lorenzo could be Navajo, Spanish, English, or Hopi in his soul. I used to watch him switch many times in as many minutes from one language and culture to another. He did it unconsciously and naturally and I don't think he was even aware that he was doing it. He switched not only languages—he spoke all four—but intonation patterns, body motions, tempo, and something additional that was impossible to define. I could see, for example, that a Hopi would talk to him in the same way he talked to people in his own village. Having grown up as a trader and knowing the people, Lorenzo was able to design his business around Indian needs and psychology, which gave him a tremendous advantage *on* the reservation with the Indians, but not necessarily *off* the reservation where he had to compete in a market not built around long-term credit of the kind he extended to his Indian customers and clients.

I found rumors, mostly from the mouths of tourists and of government employees who had read early accounts of the West, that Indian traders cheated the Indians. Undoubtedly, there were those who did. The high prices of goods may have given credence to these beliefs. But knowing what I did and watching traders operate over the years, I found these rumors hard to believe. There was the simple question of how they could do it. Prices for lambs, wool, and blankets were well known. Blankets, as we have seen, were sold by the pound, which everyone knew, and the Navajos were hard to deceive in such matters as the weight of a blanket. The only obvious way to cheat was by jiggering the scales, and some traders may have done this. All professions can count among their members individuals who are unethical, and trading was no exception. But like most businesspeople who have a close relationship with their customers, in my experience the traders were honest. During the 1930s, most complaints concerned traders violating laws set up to protect themselves from one another! It was against the law to trade anywhere except in the immediate vicinity of the store; that is, traders were not suppose to peddle. There was a reason for this, as Lorenzo explained to me. Navajos tend to be easily persuaded and have little resistance to the hard sell. By going into another trader's territory, an unscrupulous individual could obligate the Indians in that territory and then harass them to collect his debt. This amounted to unfair competition. One of the traders south of Keams had a well-deserved reputation for stealing other traders' customers, leaving the local trader holding the bag with hundreds or even thousands of dollars in uncollectible debts.

Then there were itinerant peddlers who would make forays into the reservation and undersell the local traders, skimming the thin cream of cash off the blue milk of the reservation economy. I ran into some of them when I lived briefly in Hotevilla; the peddlers lived there as well, in order to call as little attention to themselves as possible. They had no debt and virtually no overhead, and licensed traders would get apoplectic when they heard about one of these peddlers working in their backyard.

There were jokes about the butcher's thumb syndrome. Lorenzo once told me with a twinkle in his eye about a German trader named Fritz who spoke with a thick accent and, because he was not fluent in English, used a phonetic form of spelling that reflected the way he talked. It was possible to add sand to wool and blankets to make them weigh more when shipping to off-reservation warehouses. The difference was not great, but a cent or two per pound eventually added up. In Flagstaff to make a deal with the Babbitt Brothers, Fritz sent a note to his partner, who was keeping the store: "Dear Fred, Sand the wool, sand the blankets, sand the hides, and sand the money. Signed, Fritz." About a week later, a shipment of wool, blankets, and hides arrived, along with some money and a note: "Fritz, like you said, I sanded the wool, I sanded the blankets, and I sanded the hides, but doggone it Fritz, you never did show me how to sand the money. Signed, Fred." Fred didn't know it then, but the government would solve that problem fifty or sixty years later. They do it to us every day.

Few Indians were literate, and as a consequence, they developed their memories to a remarkable degree. Rigging the records of an Indian's transactions was risky business. For a big trader to have done it as a matter of policy would have been even more of a gamble. If an Indian chose not to pay a big debt and to take his business to a competitor, there was very little the first trader could do. Clearly, however, there were limits to such shenanigans; in no time the Indian would run out of gullible traders, and so much depended on long-term, personal relationships between the trader and his customers. And there was the matter of simple logistics—how far a man and his wives could afford to ride on horseback in order to trade.

It seemed to me that the traders eventually became programmed by the people they were trading with, and whether they were aware of it or not, they adopted the moral codes of their customers. The Hopis used to complain about the traders getting rich or cheating, but when pressed, the details were inevitably lacking. In fact, I knew of a case where a Hopi, going over his transactions in his head with a trader, told the trader his account was fifty cents off. The error had occurred several years earlier. It took the trader days, going over the books transaction by transaction, to prove to the Indian he had not been cheated. The cheating image will remain regardless.

Nevertheless, much of the folklore about the traders could be traced to the lack of information about the actual operations of trading stores as well as to sheer projection on the part of white tourists, who, I have observed, expect to be cheated no matter where they are in the world. That much of the business on the reservation was in trade also contributed to this image, because when a significant number of whites trade, particularly with people they see as ignorant, disadvantaged, or primitive, they often say things like, "Naturally you make the best deal you can. Besides, what does it matter, he doesn't know the true value of things. Also, his wants are simple." It is difficult to disabuse ignorant or misinformed travelers or romantic intellectuals of their misconceptions.

How much does the white man's guilt have to do with these stereotypes? A significant proportion of those who bad-mouthed the traders were from the large metropolitan

centers in the East and used a code of ethics entirely different from the one practiced in our little remnant of the
frontier. On the reservation, in the words of those times, a
man's word was still his bond. People trusted each other
and depended on each other not to take unfair advantage.
The traders were living fossils existing in a backwater. The
ethics of outsiders, who judged them, had to do with something we call progress, which may not be progress at all
but a belief in the inalienable right to make a buck at the
expense of those who can't defend themselves. This pattern
is the dynamism—the motivating power—that drives our
civilization. It was this belief that motivated the early Indian agents to try to make the Hopis into poor whites. It's
no wonder that uninformed whites were convinced that all
Indian traders were dishonest and out to squeeze every
nickel they could out of the Indians. What they didn't
know was that the Navajo system of values was powerful
and that at least some of the traders, like Chi Roberts and
the Hubbells, were converts to the Navajo way of thinking.

Much of a trader's business centered around pawn. How
he administered his pawn was as close as one could get to a
bottom-line appraisal of whether the trader had the welfare of his Indian customers at heart or not. For the most
part, however, Indian wealth was in their sheep and the
wool and the lambs they produced; the blankets woven by
the women; as well as the jewelry made by the Navajo
silversmiths. Navajo silverwork was from the beginning a
genuine Native American folk art, which was much in de-
mand. Silversmithing was first learned from the Spanish,
and the Navajo silversmiths quickly developed a high level
of skill. In general, the old sand-cast bracelets and belt
buckles were most highly prized, along with the large conchos often hammered out of Mexican pesos.

Pawned Navajo jewelry could usually be seen hanging on the wall on pegs or nails right inside the front door of the post. Each piece had a white cardboard tag attached recording the name of the owner who had pawned it, the amount for which it was pawned, and the date. The Indians would be given the end of the pawn ticket to be used when it was redeemed.

Pawn was mobile wealth. It consisted of any jewelry the Indians possessed—turquoise and silver. Each Navajo woman was bedecked in her own bracelets, rings, necklaces, concho belts, and silver buttons; many of the buttons were made out of silver quarters and ten-cent pieces, and I have seen women cut them off a blouse in order to pay the trader. The men were similarly adorned, and there was jewelry for their horses as well: bridles, cheekpieces, browbands, conchos for holding the browband to the headstall. Occasionally, a fancy bit would be taken as pawn.

The temptation was great for a trader to sell a beautiful old sand-cast bracelet to a tourist, or to an itinerant trader picking up pawn to sell to the collectors and stores in Santa Fe, or even to professional museum people bent on building up their collections. The right piece could bring many times the amount for which it was pawned, and there is no doubt that thousands of pieces of the best Navajo jewelry left the reservation during the lean depression years. Naturally, the traders knew the Indians and which pieces they valued most. Some pieces would be pawned and redeemed many times, and a few only once. The minimum limit on how long a trader had to keep a piece was six months before selling it. But even this unrealistic minimum limit (unrealistic in the sense that 180 days was too short a time for most Navajos' economic situation to change) would be breached by the more opportunistic traders. Most of the ones I knew kept pawn longer than the law required but would eventually sell it if it seemed that the Indian might not be able to redeem it. There were others like Chi Roberts, who would keep an Indian's pawn until the Indian died or moved away.

There were several reasons for displaying pawn. An Indian could come into the store and see that his jewelry was still there. Collectors on the lookout for rare pieces could tell in a few moments whether there was something they were interested in, like an old large concho belt or a particularly handsome bridle. Also, the amount of pawn was a pretty good index to the economic state of the Indians. If there was ample pawn, things were not going well. How much money was tied up in pawn would be difficult to say, but it was considerable, because thousands of dollars would be reported whenever a post was robbed.

10

The Hubbells

THE ONE HAZARD that traders did not even want to think about was robbery and with it—usually—murder. This combination was an ever-present risk.

On the evening of March 21, 1919, such a catastrophe struck Lorenzo's Uncle Charley, who ran the Hubbells' Cedar Springs store, southeast of the Hopi mesas. At the time Lorenzo was a young man a bit more than ten years into his trading career.

This was before automobiles and telephones, and when the Cedar Springs robbery and murder were discovered, an Indian runner was dispatched to Lorenzo to bring the news that the store had been robbed and burned and his uncle murdered. By the time Lorenzo reached the scene in his buckboard, almost thirty-six hours had elapsed. Approaching the scene, he saw a thin wisp of smoke rising straight up in the still air; there were lots of people—a large crowd of whites and Navajos—wagons, buckboards, and tethered horses standing around. Little remained of the trading post. Against the stark massive backdrop of the adjacent Hopi buttes, smoke still rose from the smoldering ruins. Charred, crumbling walls of sandstone were all that was left. People wandered around in a state of near shock, talking in hushed tones; other traders were relieved in their secret hearts that it had not been they and their stores. Taking this all in, Lorenzo stepped up on what was left of a crumbling wall, and arms outstretched, palms down, he said, "They did it. We will find the ones who did it. I want you all to go home."

Gradually the crowd thinned until only two Navajos remained. Kneeling down and examining the ground, they began the complex and subtle process of sorting out the tangled clues—tracks embedded in the desert soil. For almost two days, a hundred or more persons added millions of footprints in an area of roughly two acres. There is no adequate metaphor that communicates the complexity of the process in which the two trackers (Bohokishi Begay and Quinani) were engaged, for making a coherent picture of a mélange of this kind is like playing ten games of phantom chess simultaneously while blindfolded. Miraculously, they picked up a trail. Quinani walked over to Lorenzo and said, "We think we know the men who did it." Beneath all the other superimposed tracks, a pattern had emerged—two men in moccasins. From the north, two Navajos had ridden into the Dilcon/Indian Wells area at night and had broken in to the Cedar Springs store, murdered the trader after a struggle, stuffed the pawn hurriedly into saddlebags, burned the store to destroy the evidence, and quickly retreated from the contaminating, dangerous *chindi* store. Once the tracks had been read, the story was all there in the tramped grass, the broken twigs, and the sand and clay soil. All that remained was for them to backtrack the murderers to their hogans. Just in case someone was following, the killers had driven the horses back and forth over the trail and occasionally used branches from the trees to sweep the trail clean of tracks. But a short forty-eight hours later, Quinani and Bohokishi Begay found their quarry in a hogan eighty miles north of the crime scene. In the corral were five horses, three of them stolen. The imprint of the saddle blankets was still visible on the horses' backs, where sweat and pressure had flattened the hair. The ride had been a rough one, and since Navajos seldom spared their horses, these horses were tired. From the little scuff marks left on the trail, the trackers saw where the horses' feet had begun to drag from fatigue. When the trackers arrived at the hogan, they stopped, slowly dismounted, and tied their mounts in the shade of a large piñon, singing a little song so that the occupants of the hogan would know visitors were approaching. They bent down, pushed aside the skin door covering, and entered. Inside two men were squatting beside a fire, smoking, and next to them the saddlebags bulging with loot.

"It looks like you killed the Mexican trader."

"Yes, we killed him."

"Maybe you should come with us then."

That was all. In planning the crime, they had depended on white men acting like white men. Instead they were up against someone who had grown up with their own people, Lorenzo Hubbell. White men could never have sorted out the original tangled mass of footprints in the first place, nor could the white sheriffs and their deputies have been able to track their quarry over a distance of almost eighty miles. They had not counted on Lorenzo, who thought like a Navajo. Lorenzo never told me what happened to the two men—their trial or their punishment. Like his Navajo cousins, he had cleared his mind and set his mental equilibrium straight again.

When I first arrived on the reservation in 1932, J. L. Hubbell—Lorenzo's famous father—had been dead a scant two years. He had left the trading business to Lorenzo. And while Lorenzo by then had his own stores, JL's elaborate holdings in Ganado, which were being run by Lorenzo's brother, Roman, had to be integrated into the Oraibi business.

Like all the Hubbells, Roman was rotund but younger and handsomer than Lorenzo; he had a cheerful disposition and could talk about, and be talked into, almost anything. That was his problem. Also there was the matter of living up to the image of a father and an older brother who not only were national figures but could fix almost anything political, economic, and personal. While his older brother was a comprehensive thinker, Roman with his enthusiasm and active imagination could, like most of us, be distracted by the immediate demands and needs of others. The two brothers complemented each other, answering multiple needs in a wide spectrum of ever-changing situations.

Roman could be depended on to pave the way by helping outsiders who, for a variety of reasons, wanted to see Navajo ceremonies, listen to their music, make movies, or work with the Navajos as anthropologists and ethnographers. One of these, whose presence on the reservation and later professional success could be traced directly to Roman, was the anthropologist Gladys Reichard, a meticulous, dedicated field-worker. Gladys, a student of Franz Boas, was an older friend and a colleague of mine. Being a friend of Roman's, she was automatically a friend of Lorenzo's, who in announcing her arrival at Oraibi said with a grin on his face, "You're going to like Gladys—she's just like a man. She smokes a pipe and sleeps on the porch like the rest of us."

Lorenzo, like many oldtime Hispanic males, put women on a pedestal. He both romanticized and feared women and would embarrass them when he launched into his favorite laudatory discourse to the effect that "no woman could do anything that was not kind and just. No woman could be ungracious, less than beautiful, or anything but the quintessence of refinement, elegance, and grace." At this point the women who were present would become self-conscious and start to squirm and smirk. And I would sit there, no matter how many times it happened, and wonder how that man thought he could get away with such a farce. Yet the power of his presence always carried the day, and I never saw a woman challenge his view of women.

As might be surmised, Lorenzo was at ease with men but ill at ease with women. Women in those days represented a civilizing, taming, and watering-down influence on the male character. Lorenzo's life was male-oriented and male-dominated. Women were oriented toward schedules, planning, conservative views, stability, gentility, and order, none of which fitted Lorenzo's lifestyle. Women in the Spanish tradition, particularly women in the household, mothers and sisters, were sacred—above reproach and to be respected and revered above everyone else. But Ameri-

can women represented the one culture Lorenzo didn't understand and was unable to cope with. I often wondered
how a man who was so skilled in understanding and handling others could be so blind, so trapped by his own Spanish culture. In any event, he thought I would like Gladys
because you didn't have to treat her with kid gloves.

The business side of the big Hubbell post at Ganado was
presided over by the flamboyant Roman, who in turn was
supported by his pretty and gracious wife, Dorothy, who
lived in Gallup, where there were schools for their children. Lorenzo and Roman's sister, a woman I knew only
as Mrs. Goodman, managed the old Ganado home as well
as the compound around it. The Ganado trading post had
a certain charisma. It was large, square, dark, with vigas
dripping with tack, shelves heavy with goods, corners piled
high with sheepskins, and a potbellied stove in the middle.
Every time I visited, it was packed as full as an Eastern
commuter train with Navajos. Roman was always full of
ideas for making money, and Lorenzo, if he was quick
enough, would squelch these schemes with the cold light of
reality. I used to listen to him on the Oraibi end of the
telephone while Roman was explaining something to him.
Then there would be a short silence, which was not caused
by the primitive line with its crackles and pops; it was
tension. Lorenzo would shout with a combination of love
and exasperation in his voice, "My God, Roman. We can't
do that. We haven't got the *money!*" The depression was
far from over, and Lorenzo was fighting other battles to
keep his business alive.

At Ganado there was always something going on—
movie making or an entourage of big names who wanted
to see a Mountain Chant. The big shots could always be
counted on to camp at the Hubbells'. In contrast, Lo-

renzo's Oraibi post, like the man, was devoted to inner things—matters of the mind—and although it had a fair share of celebrities, they had to be the kind who penetrated appearances, who were not fooled by pretense, and who could accept what was offered—a rich experience in the simplest of surroundings.

Compared with Oraibi, a visit to Ganado was like spending a weekend at Buckingham Palace. Private rooms, real beds with clean sheets, stove lit, hot water brought by a Navajo girl in the morning, and a dining room with meals served by handsome young Navajo women. The table was ample, with a tablecloth (we had oilcloth at Oraibi) and a silver service instead of the kitchen stainless-steel, dime-store tableware at Oraibi. The china was part of a matched set. But the conversation lacked Oraibi's spontaneity and sparkle. Around the table at Oraibi you might find Lorenzo's truck drivers, an occasional Navajo headman, a government stockman, visiting scientists from Europe, an Eastern writer who was a household name, occasionally the commissioner of Indian Affairs, John Collier, or the wife of the Secretary of the Interior, Mrs. Ickes, who was well known for her deep and abiding interest in the Indians and their affairs. I heard Navajo, Hopi, Spanish, English, and French all spoken within the course of an hour in that irreverent, freewheeling atmosphere.

Mrs. Goodman was a chief presence at Ganado. She had been widowed on the afternoon of her wedding day, her husband killed in a hunting accident not far from her family's Ganado home. The wedding and lunch over, the women were in the house cleaning up while the men, gathering up their guns, set off across the fields to hunt. After a moment of happiness with thoughts of a life ahead with a loved one, it ended. She never remarried and, as far as it was known, never showed any inclination to become involved with another man.

The first time Mrs. Goodman and I were introduced—and we were formally introduced—I found myself facing an erect, dignified woman dressed in Victorian garb, who was clearly past middle age but not what you would call old. She was mistress of the Ganado household and acted as hostess first for her father, J. L. Hubbell, and later for her younger brother, Roman. Despite the air of sadness about her, there was no doubt that she was in charge, and like all the Hubbells, she exuded her own individual brand of charm and her own set of stories. One of these was about a day in Saint Johns, Arizona, during the sheep and cattle wars when all the men were away. Word came that a large group of armed men had just ridden into town. The Hubbells lived in what amounted to a fort. When there had been previous attacks, the men had been on hand and the Texas cattlemen had been driven off. This time only the women were there—Mrs. Goodman, her mother, an aunt, some adult cousins, and a few little girls.

In those days Spanish settlements were large, isolated haciendas built to be defended. The houses were built around a courtyard, facing inward so that the entrance could be blocked at a moment's notice. The haciendas had walls, barred windows, and high parapets around a roof that could be turned into a fort simply by putting armed men on it. In this event, the little girls donned men's hats and, carrying guns, marched around the roof all day. The women, also armed, stayed at the windows firing at anything that moved. All this provided enough real and apparent resistance to keep the Texans at bay. That evening the men returned, the cowboys hastily withdrew, and everyone could breathe easily again.

Cattle and sheep wars weren't the only source of mayhem in those days after the Civil War. It had not been very long since both the Indians and the Spanish had engaged in raiding each other for slaves and, no doubt, adventure. Matters did calm down, of course, but the West was still a place where disputes and differences in opinion, ethnicity, and politics were settled with guns.

Once in Lorenzo's office, I admired the garb of an old Navajo man dressed in the traditional mode of fifty years earlier—white cotton pants, Navajo buckskin moccasins, velveteen blouse, old concho belt I would have given my eyeteeth for, and bracelets to match. Standing before me was a living example of what you would see on a museum mannequin. Fletch said, "Oh yeah, he's a Mexican slave. Got his freedom twelve years ago."

"You mean to tell me that these people had slaves as recently as 1920?"

"Yeah, the Mexicans and the Navajos used to raid each other's settlements for slaves."

I would always stop at Ganado whenever I passed through on my way to or from Gallup. Once when I was about to leave, I could see that Mrs. Goodman had something on her mind. She approached and asked if I knew a Mrs. Lujan from Taos.

"Do you mean Mrs. Mabel Lujan, an Anglo lady who is married to a Taos Indian?" Having grown up from the age of eleven in Santa Fe, I knew Mabel not only as a patron of the arts and the woman who introduced D. H. Lawrence to the Southwest, but also for some of her less endearing traits. My friend Al Dasburg—the son of the famous impressionist painter Andrew Dasburg—had experienced her interference in the life of his father. She had arranged and broken three of Andrew's four marriages. Mabel's public and private sides were not the same.

"Yes. She was here last week with a man who was very interested in Navajo music. A Mr. Stokowski [Leopold Stokowski] from Philadelphia. My brother Roman went to a lot of trouble to arrange a Mountain Chant, in which Mr. Stokowski became most interested. There was a Mister Johnson in the party. I don't remember his name."

"Did they call him Spud?"

"Yes, that's it, a Mr. Spud Johnson. A small man who seemed to take care of things for Mrs. Lujan. Well, Mr. Johnson had decided that since Roman and Mr. Stokowski were involved with the Navajo medicine men and the Mountain Chant, there was time enough for him to go with the mail truck to Chinle because he had always wanted to see Canyon de Chelly. But Mrs. Lujan—I don't know why she did it—decided that they should all return to Taos. Then someone said, 'What about Spud? How's he going to get back to Taos? He doesn't have any money.' And I could tell Mrs. Lujan was a little annoyed at having to think about Mr. Johnson. She reached in her bag and took out a twenty-dollar bill and handed it to me saying, 'Give this to Mr. Johnson when he returns.' "

Mrs. Goodman then explained that she had never given money to a man in her entire life and that she had been in something of a quandary as to how to handle this breach in decorum. She put the money in an envelope, holding it hidden behind her skirt. When Spud Johnson came through the door, having noted that all the cars in Mabel's entourage were gone, he asked, "Where is everybody?"

"Mrs. Lujan decided to return to Taos." And avoiding eye contact, she turned away and handed Spud the envelope with her hand stretched out behind her, saying, "Mrs. Lujan asked me to give you this."

To which Spud replied in his usual loud, somewhat high-pitched voice, "Oh, isn't that just like Mabel. How do I get to Gallup where I can catch a bus?"

Mrs. Goodman thought the whole scene was bizarre, and when I told her that she had just witnessed the type of behavior for which Mrs. Lujan had become famous, a look of relief settled on her normally expressionless face. This was the woman who had manned the battlements against the Texas raiders.

The Hubbell entrepreneurship was nothing if not a family business. One of Lorenzo's cousins, George Hubbell, was a trader to the Navajos in Pinyon, north of the Hopi mesas and the jumping-off place where the country shifted from Hopi and Anglo influence to pure, native, indigenous, untrammeled Navajo. I never did find out exactly what George had done before Lorenzo gave him a store to run, but it had something to do with the Santa Fe Railroad in Topeka, Kansas. At any rate, it was easy to see that George had seen better times, but he never complained and made the best of a marginal situation. Shorter and even fatter than Lorenzo, George was somewhat curt, unpretentious, and utterly loyal to friends and family.

One day George arose as usual at five o'clock in the morning and stepped out on the loading dock of his store to survey the open country. To the east, clouds rose above Chinle and Canyon de Chelly some sixty miles away. Miles of sagebrush bounded by lone mesas stretched into the distance. George became aware of motion in the periphery of his vision, as four large and riderless horses appeared, walking past his store in single file, headed for Chinle. The horses were larger than Navajo mounts, so he reasoned they must belong to a white outfit. Also, they were shod, not a Navajo practice.

George ran into the store and emerged with a bucket of grain, which he shook in front of the horses, luring them into the nearby corral. He closed the gate and fetched some water for them. Around noon a Navajo on foot appeared, having tracked the horses to the corral, and went in the store to find George. There were traders and others, new to the reservation, who would simply have noted the horses passing by and done nothing except to report to the tracker that they went "thataway." Instead, George had gone to the trouble of corralling the horses and now provided the Navajo with the tack needed to lead them away to the camp, where there was a well-known writer, whom I knew and who shall remain nameless. In due course he showed up at George's trading post, where he was fed and entertained. Rather than being grateful, he later told the story of the runaway and described George (without naming him) in an article for a national magazine as "a rough and uncouth man." Somehow he thought George wouldn't read the article or that it wouldn't matter if he did. This writer never grasped the basic point: although George had not been to Harvard, he was still an important element in a delicately balanced set of hidden relationships that made the reservation function. If you couldn't understand George, you couldn't understand anything else about that country. I was mortified and embarrassed when George told me this story, and it was one of my early lessons from living on the reservation. In our journey through life, one of the first pieces of baggage to get rid of is being judgmental of others, to say nothing of putting them down.

It was a time when an entire nation was hurting in the depression and cared little for the people in this remote part of the world. My final story of the traders, the Indians, and the government, intertwined with this land in so many odd ways, is properly about Lorenzo.

One day, with my mind full of water development and dams, I drove into Keams for some supplies and found the place buzzing with excitement even more intense than usual. It seemed that the chief clerk, Keeley, had called in an inspector and that Superintendent Miller, two weeks from retirement, was about to be forced to resign in disgrace. Miller, who had served at Keams longer than any other superintendent, had been embroiled in a scandal that would cost him his job, his pension, and his reputation. It took me a while to find out what it was all about.

Miller's son evidently had a young mistress who had become pregnant. An abortion had been arranged at the Keams hospital and Keeley (who had once been reduced from the rank of superintendent to clerk for sleeping with a young Indian girl) got wind of it. It is not difficult to picture what had happened: Late at night, a door opened in the hospital on the hill above the headquarters building. A man appeared in the shaft of light—an Indian Service doctor who wanted a transfer. He and Miller made the deal in the dark. Miller had been there so long that like the captain in complete charge of his ship, he had become careless and forgot that nothing happened in Keams without everyone's knowing about it, especially the bitter Keeley.

Later that day, driving through Oraibi, I stopped off to see Lorenzo.

"What's happening?" he asked.

"Oh, the agency's in a turmoil. They are about to get Miller," I said and went on to explain. Lorenzo pressed for details.

"Who was the investigator?"

"Steelmore from Pojoaque," I said. Pojoaque was a small town north of Santa Fe. "I went to school with his son."

The next time I stopped at Oraibi, Lorenzo was gone, off on one of his unexplained trips off the reservation. I kept expecting the axe to fall on Miller at any moment. But time stretched on and to everyone's surprise and Keeley's chagrin, Miller retired without fuss or fanfare—and with his pension. The Millers came to visit Lorenzo in seclusion and then took off for Phoenix, reputation intact, no official scandal, no hearing, nothing.

Much later, when we were alone one evening, Lorenzo let drop that he could scarcely contain himself after I had spilled the beans about Miller's troubles. As soon as I left, he got into his car and drove 340 miles to Albuquerque to find out where Steelmore was at the moment. He then drove to Pojoaque, found the investigator's house in the valley and walked in.

"I understand you have a report on Superintendent Miller at Hopi."

"Yes, I just finished typing it."

"Let me see it."

Steelmore, a stolid, heavyset individual who had known Lorenzo for years, handed him the report and Lorenzo read it. While looking Steelmore in the eye, he tore up the report and threw the pieces in the wastebasket. And still fixing the inspector with a steely eye, he said as he rose to leave, "That's where it belongs and I hope it stays there."

And Miller was the one who had told me to "stay away from traders."

Epilogue

YOU MIGHT SAY that culture is the story (a myth) of
how different people place themselves in the world. And
the story, like all fairy tales, myths, and dreams, is one of
multiple levels and meanings. The Jungian Marie von
Franz says that when you destroy a people's mythology,
you destroy them. And to me that is not all. This is because
most of these myths are of the tacit variety and are not
even experienced as myths.

Our North American cultural tradition has its roots in
the wellsprings of Greek and Roman civilization. We acquired from the Greeks the idea that differing lifestyles—as
exemplified by the city-states of Athens and Sparta—were

inevitably locked in combat. Sparta's intellectual descendant, Nazi Germany, came within a hair's breadth of bringing Europe to its knees. When it became necessary for me to leave the reservation, I left behind a silent war just as desperate as our war against Hitler, a war in which the issues were even less well understood than were the distorted hopes and dreams that tied the Führer to the German people.

I had been only partially aware of the hidden, desperate tension of the reservation with its strong, vital drives pulling the reservation's inhabitants in different directions. People wrested a meager life from barren soils, living in and as part of nature, but fighting one another: progressive Hopis struggling against conservative Hopis, with the Hopi tribe striking out on all sides against whites, Navajos, the government, and change. The collective soul of a people hung in the balance. I finally began to see that just as a log can be consumed by either fire or rot (fast and slow versions of the same process), the Hopis were fighting a slow battle against degenerating forces that were destroying their life as surely as oxidation devours wood in the forest. On my last visit to Hopi country, a sign outside Old Oraibi informed me that whites were no longer welcome and were not permitted to enter the town. That was one approach. In another village, one of the more successful Hopis had his own airplane. How long will the Hopis be able to hold on to their ways? A good deal depends on how long they hold on to their language. One avenue, of course, is for some of their members to begin to study, analyze, and record, not just the conscious side of their culture but the tacit dimensions as well. There is incredible strength in Hopi culture. And there are people in the world who could use some of that strength.

The more flexible and more adaptive Navajos treated change and the engulfing Western technology differently. Either way, like a field of mountain snow on a bright June day, the old life of both cultures was melting away.

Just as there is a complex interface between the sun and the snow, I have always thought that the secrets of human existence are to be found at the interface between peoples. The American psychoanalyst Harry Stack Sullivan was one of the first to make significant note of this in what he termed *transactions* between people. Sullivan's world was an *interpersonal* world in which each of the major components and patterns is seen as a transaction. On the reservation, I was already getting my first lesson in transactional psychology. The transactional approach contrasts the cause and effect of group interaction with the more conventional view of single causes and single effects, which result in people attempting to find fault with, and fix blame on, a particular individual. The reader may well ask, "What does all this have to do with what happened to the Hopis?"

Viewed from the transactional perspective, it isn't enough to say that the whites in charge were wrong, even cruel at times. To do so is to remain trapped in our own cultural shell, still trying to fix guilt and innocence in a dichotomizing way based on our own cultural biases. Because they were living within the bounds of their own cultures, neither the Hopis nor the white officials could be characterized as anything but sane. It was the transaction between them that was insane and it was this insanity that really got to me. There was something about Hopi culture that seemed to drive the Indian agents wild, bringing out the very worst possible responses in them.

I didn't realize it at the time, but I arrived on the scene at the end of an era of blatant colonialism during which two lifestyles were fighting it out—each in its own way, trying to make the other "cry uncle." There is a defect, however, in pinning labels on people and events. The defect is assuming that men like Superintendents Lemmon, Crane, and Daniel could control and change Hopi behavior any more than the Hopi chiefs like Youkioma and Tewaquaptewa of Old Oraibi could change the white man. But even if those white archaic types were incapable of changing themselves, there were people in charge at higher levels of government who should have known better. Basic attitudes and their associate behaviors change slowly. For example, in 1949 I was asked to write a chapter on "world" history for writers and professors of history. My opening comments were to the effect that what we were calling world history was actually a history of European civilization, including its roots in the Middle East. The rest of the world had been left out. In addition, nothing was said about women; and world history was the history of war, which happened to be primarily a male pursuit. What was being taught in our schools, colleges, and universities was loaded with unstated, unconscious biases. It is these widely shared biases of the unconscious that direct events with an iron hand. I should mention that we are not alone in this regard; all cultures suffer from this type of corruption of the perceptual process. One cannot change the past, we can only put the past in a wider frame.

Nevertheless, all peoples have their heroes and villains. Sometimes history shows the heroes to have really been villains and vice versa. All peoples know individuals who are known to be wise and kind and others who are self-centered and mean. All peoples provide for themselves a spectrum of responses to crises. It is the process by which a crisis is handled, the rules by which life is lived, and the *language* of behavior that differ from one culture to the next. When cultures meet and start interacting with each other, *even well-chosen words may not be enough to bridge the cultural gap.*

If we view our government's treatment of the Hopis (using this example as a case type) in retrospect, it should be clear that the human species would be well advised to assign only those who are wise and kind to conduct the difficult and sensitive business of intercultural relations, particularly when dealing with people who are less powerful *politically.* Lives are frequently worlds apart, and it takes wisdom and patience to bridge such gaps. The story that unfolded over the years on the reservation left me with the conviction that the power and force of culture cannot be, nor should be, repressed. It is the drive to keep ourselves comfortable by making others transform themselves into clones of ourselves that is so destructive. This is doubly so when we are not even aware of it.

The drive to control our own inputs seems to be even stronger than the sexual drive. People can on occasion do without sex, but they have a more difficult time avoiding the temptation to put down another culture, to the extreme of "cultural cleansing." This is particularly true if those others can't fight back. Of course, if we look at people as underdeveloped or primitive, or at a less advanced stage than we have achieved, it is easy to rationalize molding them in our own image, since we believe we are "doing them a favor."

The first of such dubious favors endured by the Hopis was in the 1600s when the Franciscan Brothers at Awatovi and Shongopavi imposed their religion on the Hopis. The Spanish looked down on the Hopis as savages, and it is a matter of historical record that the Brothers enslaved many of the Hopis, forcing them to haul water to the mesa tops to water fruit trees and gardens, forcing them to build churches and dwellings and to cut wood—in a word, to do all the things that slaves do. How do I know about these things and how the Hopis felt? Because the Hopis were still complaining bitterly about how mean the Spanish were to them three hundred years after the fact. The ill will generated by the Spanish caused the Hopis to join the Pueblo Revolt in 1680 and to hang the priests and destroy the churches at Awatovi and Shongopavi. This situation of receiving and rejecting the white man's religion was the foundation on which the "friendly" and the "hostile" factions were built.

As an outsider sensitive to verbal as well as nonverbal behavior, I soon discovered that even when dealing with the friendlies, who were eager to be acknowledged, Hopi culture and Anglo culture meshed only on the most superficial levels. The deeper I went, the farther apart the two cultures became. This is why I thought it important to take a look—albeit a brief, uncomplicated one—at the inner Hopi, because it is the inner Hopi that proved to be more real. When I speak of the inner Hopi, I am simply referring to that part I have spent half a century studying in my own people's transactions with one another as well as with peoples of other cultures of the world. This is the behavioral equivalent of language before it has been analyzed and reduced to writing.

My point is this: *In order to understand a transaction, one must be able to see and understand both sides of the equation.*

I didn't leave the reservation all at once. In 1936 and 1937, I worked as a dendrochronologist for the Peabody

Museum on its excavations of the town of Awatovi. I also spent a season in the northernmost part of the reservation, from Kayenta north to Navajo Mountain and Rainbow Bridge.

The last time I saw Lorenzo he had gotten married—against the advice of everyone. The mammoth coffeepot that never left the kitchen stove was replaced with, as Lorenzo expressed it, "its little brother." I always thought that the marriage was in response to pressures other than libidinal and that it was Lorenzo's way of putting a period at the end of his life's work. In poor health, he died in March 1942. Later, I found a letter postmarked Oraibi, April 1, in my mailbox in Santa Fe. Opening it, I saw Lorenzo's letterhead. It was from his brother, Roman, and read as follows:

Dear Ned:

I've been sitting here in Lorenzo's office at Oraibi and wishing that Lorenzo was the one that was writing you this letter. I am sure that what I have to suggest to you would be very much what Lorenzo would like. I know what dear friends you were. I know you will miss him as well as thousands of Indians and whites.

E. R. Fryer,* I understand, is temporarily leaving Window Rock and is going to have something to do with the problem that confronts the state of Arizona around Parker for the interned Japanese. I would love to see you put in Fryer's place, not only temporarily, but permanently. If you are interested in this, why not write to Collier and pull some strong strings to accomplish this?

* *Fryer was superintendent of the new consolidated Navajo agency at Window Rock, Arizona.*

Your understanding of the Indian problems and your insight into their nature and the human feeling that you have for all mankind suits you to this position. I really know down in my heart that you would like to help the Navajos, and God knows they need a friend.

Amigo,

signed (Roman)

It was a romantic and an entirely impractical idea, typical of Roman, and a wonderful compliment. But in 1942, the world was cracking with gunfire, and I was in the process of moving onto a larger stage.

As it did to many men in the 1940s, World War II ripped me forcibly out of my Southwestern context, bringing everything in my life to a precipitous halt. My Army experience reconstituted not only my life but my personality. The war, also, put a period on the closing sentence of nineteenth-century life on the reservation.

After the war, roads were paved, and the big washes—Steamboat, Wepo, Oraibi, Dinnebito, and Moenkopi—were all bridged. Prosperity came to the reservation, bringing four-wheel-drive vehicles and pickup trucks instead of wagons and horses for the Navajos and the Hopis. There was also the Peabody Coal Company ripping the guts out of Black Mesa, and Lake Powell providing access to tourists by the thousands to the once inaccessible Rainbow Bridge. In the Four Corners region, giant power plants produced electricity to light Phoenix and Los Angeles, and the smog choked the Grand Canyon and obscured the view of Mount Taylor, halfway between Santa Fe and Gallup. Because all the new roads brought more and more people, the National Park Service had to control access to Canyon de Chelly and the great ruins of Betatakin and Keit Seil. Lorenzo Hubbell's trading post at Oraibi was torn down after his death in 1942, and the Hubbell empire collapsed and eventually went into receivership. Fortunately, the Hubbell post at Ganado is now a national historic site, and there is a move to make the Hubbell store and warehouses in Winslow a state monument.

One advantage of age is that occasionally one is lucky enough to see things change for the better and, as a consequence, to get a feeling for change in a much broader perspective. I am not an economic determinist, but having observed my own people from the Great Depression through four wars, in affluence and inflation, I am convinced that money seldom buys happiness. Living at the very edge of survival, however, as the Hopis did, can have a devastating effect on human beings. Some of the affluence of Western society that has spilled over on the Hopis has had a beneficial effect, whether they acknowledge it or not. Relative prosperity has made a big difference in their lives. The dogs I saw on my most recent visit were sleek and filled out. No longer are there blind old men, eyes white with cataracts, sitting outdoors in the winter sun, unable to move more than a few feet. Gone are the younger people of both sexes with conjunctivitis and their corneas inflamed and scarred by trachoma. A few drops of diluted silver nitrate in the eyes at birth eradicate this disease. Gone are the pustular eruptions on Hopis' faces from a particularly virulent form of impetigo.

The lesson of the Hopis is compelling only if one comprehends and takes into account their history, the experiences with drought and starvation they have suffered, and how these events molded their behavior and their perceptions.

The highly structured character of Hopi life was an asset, for they have weathered the typhoon of European culture and managed to hold on to their own. Paved roads and automobiles (even their own airplanes) have changed things. But then that is the nature of life. The story of our species is a book of change without end.

Selected Readings

AMSDEN, CHARLES. *Navaho Weaving*. New York: Dover, 1990.

CARROLL, JOHN B., ed. *Language, Thought, and Reality: Selected Writings of Benjamin Lee Whorf*. Cambridge: MIT Press, 1956.

COLLIER, JOHN. *Indians of the Americas*. New York: Norton, 1947.

COLTON, HAROLD S. *Hopi Kachina Dolls with a Key to their Identification*. Albuquerque: University of New Mexico Press, 1987.

DYK, WALTER. *Son of Old Man Hat: A Navaho Autobiography*. Lincoln: University of Nebraska Press, 1967.

DYK, WALTER, and RUTH DYK. *Left-Handed: A Navaho Autobiography*. New York: Columbia University Press, 1980.

JAMES, HARRY C. *Pages from Hopi History*. Tucson: University of Arizona Press, 1974.

KABOTIE, FRED. *Fred Kabotie: Hopi Indian Artist*. Flagstaff: Museum of Northern Arizona, 1977.

KENNARD, EDWARD H. *Hopi Kachinas*. Locust Valley, N.Y.: Augustin, 1938.

KLUCKHOHN, CLYDE, and DOROTHEA LEIGHTON. *The Navajo*. Cambridge: Harvard University Press, 1973.

MCNITT, FRANK. *The Indian Traders*. Norman: University of Oklahoma Press, 1989.

MARRIOTT, ALICE. *The Ten Grandmothers*. Norman: University of Oklahoma Press, 1983.

MOMADAY, N. SCOTT. *House Made of Dawn.* New York: HarperCollins, 1966.

NEWCOMB, FRANC JOHNSON. *Hosteen Klah.* Norman: University of Oklahoma Press, 1972.

ORTIZ, ALFONSO, vol. ed. *Handbook of North American Indians Southwest.* Vols. 9 and 10. Washington, D.C.: Smithsonian Institution, 1979, 1983.

PAGE, JAKE, and SUZANNE PAGE. *Hopi.* New York: Abrams, 1982.

REICHARD, GLADYS ALICE. *Navajo Religion: A Study of Symbolism.* Princeton, N.J.: Princeton University Press, 1990.

———. *Navaho Shepherd and Weaver.* Glorieta, N.Mex.: Rio Grande Press, 1984.

———. *Spider Woman: A Story of Navajo Weavers.* Glorieta, N.Mex.: Rio Grande Press, 1968.

SILKO, LESLIE MARMON. *Ceremony.* New York: Viking Penguin, 1986.

SIMMONS, LEO W., ed. *Sun Chief: The Autobiography of a Hopi Indian.* New Haven, Conn.: Yale University Press, 1963.

WATERS, FRANK. *Book of the Hopi.* New York: Viking Penguin, 1977.

WEBB, WILLIAM, and ROBERT A. WEINSTEIN. *Dwellers at the Source: Southwestern Indian Photographs of A. C. Vroman, 1895–1904.* Albuquerque: University of New Mexico Press, 1987.

Index

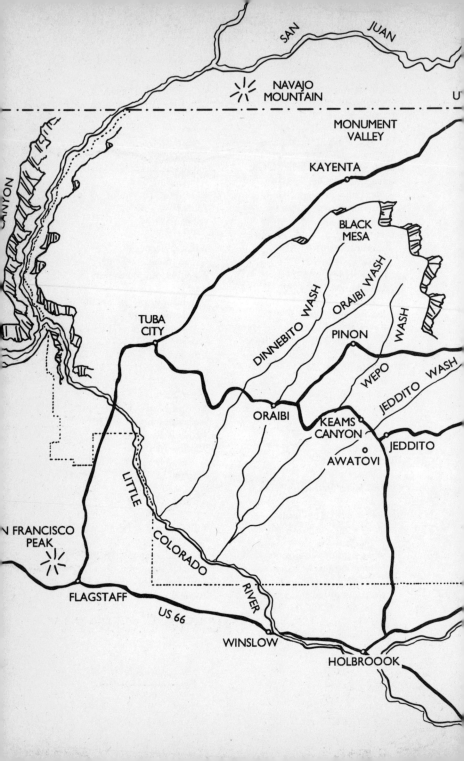

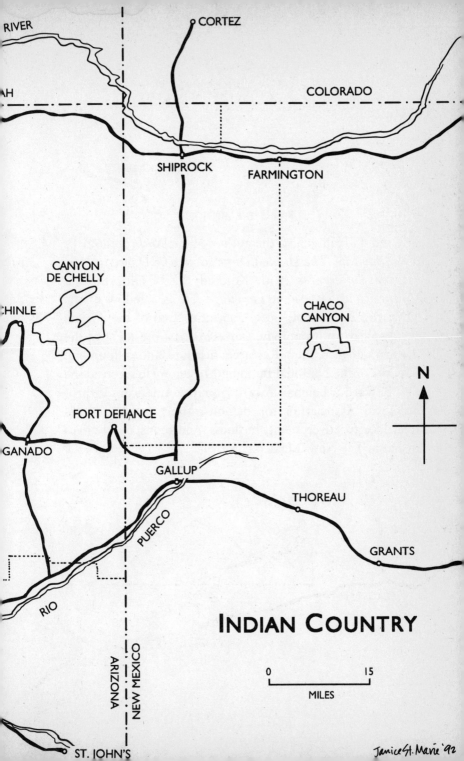

Edward T. Hall is also the author of *An Anthropology of Everyday Life*, *The Hidden Dimension*, *The Dance of Life*, *Hidden Differences* (with Mildred Reed Hall), *Beyond Culture*, and *The Silent Language*. He is a fellow of the American Anthropological Association and of the Society for Applied Anthropology, as well as past president of the Anthropological Film Research Institute and a founding director of the National Building Museum. He received the first Edward J. Lehman Award from the American Anthropological Association for demonstrating anthropology's relevance to government, business, and industry. He lives in Santa Fe, New Mexico.